RUBBER SIDE DOWN

Road Dog Publications was formed in 2010 as an imprint dedicated to publishing the best in books on motorcycling and adventure travel. Visit us at www.roaddogpub.com.

ISBN 978-1-890623-74-6
Library of Congress Control Number: 2022946397

An Imprint of Lost Classics Book Company

This book also available in eBook format at online booksellers.
ISBN 978-1-890623-75-3

RUBBER SIDE DOWN

THE IMPROBABLE INCLINATION TO
TRAVEL ON TWO WHEELS

by

Ron Davis

Publisher
Lake Wales, Florida

Also by Ron Davis
Shiny Side Up: Musings on the Improbable
Inclination to Travel on Two Wheels

If you're in the market for a light and unpretentious read that says half of the things you're thinking and written from the perspective of a rider who truly knows his stuff, then do yourself a favor and pick up a copy of Ron's book. —WebBikeWorld

If you're looking for a light read about motorcycles, the riding lifestyle and growing old gracefully, check out Shiny Side Up by BMW fan Ron Davis. —Motorbike Writer

...an excellent read for a rider who is not on the road like he or she wishes to be. —Backroads Motorcycle Magazine

What would Peter Egan the maestro of motorcycle columns, think about another Wisconsin motorcycle editor riding down the same path and booking up his magazine columns. In fact, the dean of motorcycle writers has already provided his review: 'A great collection of columns, and they make it hard to turn your reading light off and go to bed. It is one of those "Just one more" books, a fun mixture of humor and insight that'll resonate with anyone who rides.'" —Bruce Curie for RoadRunner Touring and Travel Magazine

Jack Riepe is a fan of Ron's and I am, too. If you like the writing of Peter Egan (also a fan), you'll like the writing of Ron Davis. —Tom Van Horn for BMW Owners News

Ron Davis is a longtime motorcycle industry veteran with years of experience waxing poetic about the two-wheeled lifestyle...Those looking for some light reading after a ride should pick up a copy. —Rider Magazine

ABOUT THE AUTHOR

Ron Davis caught the motorcycle bug at age fifteen. Forty years and about twenty bikes later, he has remained an enthusiast, especially for bikes carrying the BMW roundel. Over that period, he's also squeezed in a full-time career teaching high school and university classes in writing, photography, and publishing, while also working as a social media writer for the tourism industry in Northwest Ontario and as an associate editor and columnist for *BMW Owners News*. More often tongue-in-cheek commentary than a technical or travel focus, his writing has been featured by *BMW Motorcycle Magazine, On The Level, Backroads Motorcycle TourMagazine, Volume One, Our Wisconsin*, and the *National Writing Project*, and his essays (some about riding) can be heard regularly on Wisconsin Public Radio's "Wisconsin Life." His first book, like this one, is a compilation of columns, essays, and features with some connection to the motorcycle life; however, *Rubber Side Down* also includes not only new motorcycling stories, but reviews, personality profiles, and a few memoirs. Ron said, "One of the most gratifying responses I heard to *Shiny Side Up* was that you didn't have to be a motorcyclist to enjoy it. I hope that's even more true with this second volume."

CONTENTS

About the Author

RUBBER SIDE DOWN

1

REALLY TRUE TRUTHS

Misinformation, disinformation, alternate facts, fake news . . . Isn't there anything we can regard as "true" anymore? And if so, where can you find some of this truth-i-ness? Well, fortunately, I'm here, and you can trust me when it comes to truth-telling. Unfortunately, the only thing I know anything about is motorcycling. To borrow the immortal line from Spandau Ballet, I know this much is true . . .

1.   All motorcyclists will have at some time noticed that his or her turn signal has been on for the last five miles.

2.   All stock seats suck.

3.   That tickle you feel under your helmet? Yes, that's a spider.

4.   Attempting to explain "desmodromic" is never a good idea at a cocktail party.

5.   Coffee will always taste better around a campfire; a beer will always taste better after a 350 mile day.

6.   It will rain. It will be cold. It will be hot. It may even snow. However, you will often meet the nicest people while sheltering under an overpass, at a convenience store, or at a wayside.

7.   It may take years to find a riding buddy who likes the same pace you do.

8.   No matter how many bikes or how many other brands are in the parking lot, BMWs will always get respect.

9.   No one has ever removed and then re-installed fairings and all the other plastic bits without discovering a bolt or screw left over.

10.   During four out of five stops for gas you will be approached by someone who will ask how you like your bike, where you are headed, etc., then tell you about their personal history with motorcycles. It will not be an unpleasant conversation.

11.   No, that driver doesn't see you.

12.   You will drop your bike.

13.   Somehow, taxes, title, prep, license, insurance, and accessory costs never seem to come up when discussing the purchase of a new bike with your spouse.

14.   When you walk into work and it's ten degrees below outside, invariably someone will ask, "Ride the bike today?" (Thank you, Andy Goldfine.)

15.   There are roughly 2,110 interpretations of the rules governing roundabouts.

16.   There is no such thing as a "universal motorcycle."

17.   Without fail, sometime, somewhere, there will be a washout of sand, gravel, or manure awaiting you just over the crest of the next hill.

18.   It's probably best to avoid using Jon Delvecchio's phrase *kissing the mirror* around those who haven't read his book.

19.   Two motorcycles are always better than one, three better than two, etc.

20. You will only miss a shift, stall your bike, or forget to put the sidestand up when other riders are watching.

21. When adding an accessory to your bike, rarely will it install as easily or work as seamlessly as advertised.

22. You will always have at least one close call whenever you decide it's too hot or too inconvenient for riding gear.

23. You will forget motel rooms; you will remember campsites.

24. When you stop for a sandwich, you'll always sit where you can see your bike.

25. Drivers in turn-only lanes have a habit of choosing other options.

26. You will only remember your ear plugs after your helmet is strapped on.

27. Your gloves/boots/ear plugs/phone/keys will always be in the last place you look.

28. Your panniers will never be quite big enough, nor will your garage.

29. Tires will never last as long as you think they should.

30. The number one motorcycle accessory is a cell phone.

There's no doubt about it, sometimes the truth hurts, and accepting truths like these can be startling, embarrassing, even painful, but with each ride, and with it, each revelation, don't we all become a little more careful, a little more deliberate, and I have to hope, a little wiser? Now, what's the rule about roundabouts? Oh, yeah, yield to traffic from the left!

The Recapture Lodge, Bluff, Utah

2
Even More "Truth-i-ness"

After I wrote a column called "Really True Truths" (BMW Owners News, August, 2021). It occurred to me that there is probably an unlimited number of additions that could be made to that list, including, "Sometimes the best 'Global Positioning System' is a five-dollar army surplus compass." Since the column was published, I also received a number of suggestions for additions that seem just as "truth-y" as anything I wrote:

"You will forget chain motel rooms; you will remember mom-and-pop places (like Recapture Lodge in Bluff, Utah, and what is now the Stargazer Inn in Baker, Nevada)—Randy Bishop

"Save everything! The week after you finally throw out that twenty-year-old weird metal scrap, you'll realize it would serve perfectly as an improvised part or special tool." And "Abandon logic when looking for small parts you drop in the garage. Begin your search efforts in dark, impossibly distant crevices, where you're absolutely certain they could never reach while in Earth's gravitational field."—Mark Barnes

"A family member will always comment on how great a day it is for a ride when you're entertaining and feeding them and cleaning up after them at your house. Then it rains the next day and the next weekend."—Bob Hasiuk

"No matter what you wear, I suspect you'll be on either side of comfortable all day long."—Peter Egan, from a comment made by Allan Girdler while deciding what jacket to wear for a multi-bike test trip.

"If not now, when?" Recalled from an issue of *Backroads Magazine* ten years ago about a High Alps tour by Stephen Pittman IV. He wrote, "We went. Heck of a trip!" He also added:
"Always wave at kids in the car next to you."
"Even if you have the right of way, don't take it."
"Go around that puddle."
"Get off the Interstate."

Ken Hollis had a few:
"Buy a retractable claw retriever stick, because that bolt you JUST removed/tried to install will fall into the tiniest space possible where it cannot be reached by human hands."
"No matter how much you plan your trip in detail, look at the weather forecast for the day; when you finish your day it will be different than you thought . . . But that is the GOOD part of riding."
"It's easier to replace a jacket than get a skin graft."
"The only way to ensure you stay dry and warm when you ride is to have a really big garage."

"You will forget to zero the odometer at the last fuel stop and make a gloved attempt to dial it back while underway until you come to your senses as to the foolishness of the effort."—Stuart Stebbings

"You will only get stuck in traffic when it's blistering hot or raining." And "You will always wonder what caliber the last bug strike was."—Steve Draher

And of course, not to be outdone, Jack Riepe graciously put down his Negroni and shared some wisdom from his most recent book:

"That noise coming from the engine is the sound of $2,500 changing hands at the closest dealer."

"A $400 microchip will gladly sacrifice its life for a $2 fuse."

"That woman you met in the bar last night—the one who loves motorcycles?—loves all of them except yours."

"The glue in your tire patch kit is inversely viscous to the distance you are from an auto parts store."

"The best flat prevention is carrying a CyclePump and an EZAir tire gauge for fifteen years."

"That state-of-the-art tent you bought fifteen years ago will dissolve like an Alka Seltzer tablet in a light mist the first time you talk a date into spending the night with you."

Thanks to all who sent kind comments and additions to my list!

1959 Royal Enfield Indian Chief

3

PRIDE GO-ETH
BEFORE THE FALL

It was 1966, and I was king of the world. As an eighth grader, I was among the oldest kids in the school. I had pretty much seen it all, and nobody, not even the teachers, pushed me or my buddies around. And those buddies, they were popular, they were smart, got good grades (even if I didn't), and they all wore Beatle boots. I wrote for the school newspaper (What did S.H. give S.R. in the L.C.?!!), and of course, I had a girlfriend.

The girlfriend? The previous summer, a girl wearing a white sailor cap and blue cat's eye glasses started showing up at every one of my baseball games (I was a catcher and the stat leader on base-on-balls). She even started riding back and forth in front of my house on her bike. "Who's that little girl in the sailor hat?" my mom, ever all-knowing, would ask. But it wasn't until the Halloween dance that I made my move. Donna walked up and asked me to dance (it was a slow one), and to my friends' jealous snickering, I did. Soon, she and I were going steady, which at that time basically meant a lot of time on the phone, Cokes at Arndt's Restaurant after Saturday morning ball games, some sweaty hand-holding, and a few nervous kisses.

Donna and I got along fine, but by spring, at the very zenith of my ascendency, I was starting to feel a little tied down. The high school I would be going to in the fall had over 2,000 students, and even with my negligible math skills, I figured maybe half had to be girls, a good number of them possibly worthy of me. So, obviously, it was time to dump Donna.

As I remember, it wasn't a very gracious dumping. My friend, Steve, volunteered to call her. We hadn't rehearsed anything, and he began by screwing up: "Ron says he makes you sick, I mean, you make him—I mean—He hates your guts!" My buddies, grouped around the phone, burst into hysterics, and Steve beamed triumphantly as he slammed the phone down. I was in shock. I wanted to dump Donna, not destroy her! But all was soon forgotten as we trooped outside and across Main Street to impress all the girls at the Dairy Queen by chugging slurppies and riding our Schwinns no-handed.

When high school started the next fall, it turned out my kingly reign was over. I went into the wrong classroom on the first day; I couldn't crack the combination on my locker so was left carrying all my books around, only to have them repeatedly knocked to the floor by letter-jacketed mouth breathers. And worst, as I forlornly walked out of school at the end of the day, I was stunned to see a sinister-looking, black Royal Enfield Indian Chief rumble by with Donna on the back, her arms wrapped lasciviously around the chest of some guy in engineer boots and James Dean sunglasses.

I huddled with my buddies in my friend Steve's bedroom to commiserate over our sad fates, and somebody mentioned he had seen Donna wearing a class ring as big as a deuce and a half lug nut hanging on a chain between her breasts. What a slut. Actually, those were my exact words, overheard in the next room, incidentally, by Steve's younger sister, who, incidentally, was a good friend of Donna.

The next day in school, I was determined to work on restoring my image. I had figured out that I didn't need to carry all my books for all my classes all day long. I learned how to jam my locker, so I didn't have to worry about the combination. I had also picked up a pristine copy of *Cycle World* to drool over. Things were looking up, and by the end of fifth hour Algebra, I was feeling a faint glimmer of confidence as I headed into the swirling mass of high school humanity at the intersection of the school's two main hallways.

A statue of Old Abe himself presided up on a pedestal at the crossroads, painted gold and staring off toward the cafeteria, as if intrigued with the wafting scent of tuna casserole. As I scanned the crowd marching by on the left, I spotted Donna approaching (sans biker boyfriend). Her glasses were gone, her culottes were hemmed right at the dress code limit, and she wore a madras blouse with a couple buttons open at the top. Not being one to ever give up on my options, I turned on the full candlepower of my charm, grinned at Donna, and did a casual wave. To my surprise, she steered toward me. Second thoughts?

However, just as we met, her face grew hard, her eyes narrowing. I began to say a cheerful "Hi!" when suddenly she brought her right hand up in a swift uppercut to my jaw. In her hand she had been holding a leather clutch purse containing, I surmised later, a few rolls of quarters. Her shot lifted me off my feet, and the next thing I knew I was lying flat on my back at Abe and Donna's feet, a crowd of onlookers hovering in around us.

Donna leaned down into my dazed vision and hissed through clenched teeth, "If you're going to talk behind someone's back, you better be careful what you say!" There was laughter and applause from the crowd as Donna stalked off in triumph, while I, on hands and knees, struggled to gather up my books, glasses, and, oh yes, a powder blue pencil case, which was by then being kicked down the hall.

Twenty-five years and five motorcycles later, I ran into Donna at a class reunion. I reminded her about the fateful punch she had given me, but strangely, she had no recollection of my insult, the purse, or unbelievably, us even going steady! I can only conclude that she was either lying out of embarrassment and regret or that there had possibly been so many victims of that ten pound purse that their individual memories had become blurred. Yeah, she was probably lying.

2019 BMW G 310 GS

4

BACK TO THE FUTURE

Anyone who's read my column over the years knows I have a nostalgic affinity for small, simple bikes, a congenital disease that demands buying something new every few years, and foremost, an aversion to prying open my wallet (okay, I'm cheap). Those three qualities had a lot to do with my interest in BMW's G 310 GS ever since its launch in 2016. Finally, this past summer (not in small part due to Jocelin Snow's face-off story between the 1250 and 310 GS), I hiked up to BMW Motorcycles of Richfield for a look-see and a demo ride.

It turned out the dealership had a bunch of the 310s, both the R and GS models, but they were going fast, due to a $500 incentive expiring at the end of July. Although Richfield's salesperson had apparently not then yet heard of it, he was also willing to honor the $250 MOA discount, making a deal sound even sweeter.

Swinging a leg over the diminutive GS after owning 700 and 1150 models, I was surprised how it didn't feel like a downsized bike, my 5'9" frame fit just fine. On the demo ride, confirming what I already knew, the 313cc engine was not a head snapper and provided a little more anxiety for pulling out into traffic than I was used to. But, tooling around parking lots, suburban streets, and four lane highways, the flickability and lighter weight took me back to what first attracted me to motorcycles, namely, riding was a blast!

Unlike BMWs Gelände/Straße 750s, 850s, and 1250s, the *S* from the GS in the 310's model name should stand for "simplicity." Switchable ABS was the only concession to the larger bikes' plethora of alphabet rider aides like ASC, DTC, and all the other incomprehensible alphabetic combinations BMW has dreamed up. There are no tire pressure monitors or ambient temp gauge, no heated grips, and no self-canceling turn signals. In many ways, this is an old-school, just-get-out-and-have fun bike. True, the brakes are modern, with a radial-mounted caliper on the front disc; the gorgeous gold forks are inverted; the fuel gauge is an improvement over the F700's; and the cylinder's backward tilt is certainly innovative, but the bike still felt basic with a *B*, which frankly didn't bother me a bit.

After the ride, I did cast a longing eye toward the new 750s beckoning from the Richfield showroom floor, but then it dawned on me I could buy TWO 310s for the cost of one 750! I sat down with Jerry, the Aussie sales manager, to look at some numbers. With some figures scrawled onto a business card, I crawled out of the construction zone otherwise known as Minneapolis, mulling the prospect that this might be my next bike.

A few days later, after taking a somewhat imprecise scan of my bank account, I rented a trailer and headed back to Minneapolis. As it turned out, my daughter went into labor with her first child the same morning, but well, you know, there was that incentive about to expire and . . .

Now, a month or so later (Mom and 9 lb. 14 oz. baby Lincoln doing fine), I'm ready to make a few fairly specific judgements on what should definitely not be called "The Baby GS." Braking: at first I felt like the 310's brakes were soft, but after the brake pads seated, they became considerably firmer. Still not the bite of my 700, but fine for a bike this light.

Shifting/Power: The bike is geared low, so thinking about fourth at 35 mph takes some getting used to. As I've gotten more accustomed to revving the bike much higher than I would on a larger bike (which is where its power lies), I'm getting better at squeezing enough out of a third of a liter to feel comfortable in traffic, although shifting does keep you busy. (The dash, surprisingly, DOES have a gear indicator.) Power I'd term "adequate," which is fine with me, and the 70 mpg is an attractive trade-off. Also, I've got to admit the sound of this bike in the +5K range is kinda gnarly!

Ergonomics: As I indicated earlier, the bike does not feel small to me. The seat is surprisingly comfortable, at least for an hour or so, and although highway speeds feel buzzy (55-65 is no problem), adding some Original Grip Buddies and probably a set of Rox handlebar risers will probably help with hand fatigue.

Handling: The little GS is definitely flickable, feels sure-footed in the corners, and keeps a steady track at high speed, although I haven't been in any big wind yet. Though it would break my heart to drop it, as a 175-pound weakling I have no worries about picking it up.

Farkling: It's a basic bike, and I plan to try to keep it that way. I'm a windshield guy, I so did add a Givi windscreen, and the tiny sidestand foot definitely demands an aftermarket plate. Unlike the R model, the 310 GS comes with a rear rack, so I bolted on a small Pelican-like case for possibles, and I found a cool set of expandable, dual-sport saddle bags from Nelson-Rigg that work just fine. If I should need more storage, I'll strap on my well-worn Aerostich Courier Bag. Front auxiliary lights would be nice, but only if they're something unobtrusive. Otherwise, I'm working on restraint.

Looks: It's been a month, and I'll admit I still can't walk past the bike without ogling it for a few moments. The GS beak, the ADV humped tank, the gold forks, the white monoshock, the upswept can, the usual clean lines of a BMW—it's a pretty bike.

At this stage in my riding career, I'm no longer enthused about butt burners or even hops much farther than visiting my grandkids an hour away. Tooling around town, slicing through some Driftless Area county trunks are in this bike's sweet spot. A few years ago, I wrote a story with the headline, "For Every Bike There Is A Time," and this seems to be my time for the BMW G 310 GS.

1975 Honda CB200

5
THREE CHRISTMASES

Christmas One

A Christmas morning more than twenty years ago found my daughter playing Santa, handing out gifts one by one. I was mystified when she brought me a box large enough to hold a basketball. It was from my wife, but I could tell from the way the entire family stopped whatever they were doing, they all knew what I would find inside: a shiny black, full-face motorcycle helmet. I had not owned a motorcycle in fifteen years.

My wife knew what she was doing. She'd seen the way any kind of bike passing by always riveted my attention, watched me devour piles of bike magazines, and noticed how my face would light up whenever a buddy brought over his Honda Scrambler for me to take a short spin. The helmet was a cheap one, but it was more a symbol, tacit approval to become a rider again.

Two weeks later, my buddy, Ralph, and I were on a trek to Hudson, Wisconsin, where, through eBay, I had found a 1975 Honda CB200. Despite its age, it had less than 500 miles on the odometer. The owner told me he and his son, both riders, had bought the bike for his wife, so she could learn. She made one trip around the block then took a spill as she turned into the driveway, where she announced she wanted nothing more to do with motorcycles.

Since then, the little Honda mostly had just sat. I knew it would take some work to make it roadworthy again—new tires and battery, carbs and gas tank cleaning, and probably new points and plugs—but it was still only January, and the 200 seemed like a good re-start to the cycle of life. It actually started, and after running up and down the driveway, we were able to lift the bike into back of my pickup.

Christmas Two

Thirty or forty years before that day, again on a Christmas morning, I was around seven years old and was eagerly watching the same routine, one member of the family handing out our gifts to each other. Beside my usual anticipation for my own gifts, I was especially interested in watching my sisters, brother, mom, and dad open theirs, because this was the Christmas I had decided to make all my gifts myself.

My dad was getting a flour and water ashtray that suspiciously resembled a likeness of a moon crater I had made for school, my sister was getting a ring toss game of mason jar rings and pieces of a broomstick (she was then sixteen), but it was my mother's I was most proud of. The project started with a glimpse of a gift idea in *Boy's Life*. It was a pencil holder, made to be hung conveniently near a calendar or telephone, carved and painted to look like a carrot. However, in my abundant seven-year-old wisdom, and not any more of stickler for details than I am now, I had surmised a real carrot would work just as well. So, secretly whittling out the center of a good-sized carrot and drilling out two holes with a tooth pick for a string (although I figured a rubber band would work just as well) my masterpiece was complete.

To disguise the true nature of my mother's gift, I wrapped it in an old shoe box—all my "shopping" for the family done with more than three weeks to spare! In the days leading up to Christmas, I took particular delight in my mom's puzzlement when she shook her present, even urging my dad to take a turn. That poor carrot.

After what seemed like centuries, Christmas morning finally arrived. Even in the midst of tearing open all the treasures I was receiving, I kept an ear cocked for the signs of appreciation for the gifts of my arduous labor. As my mother opened the lid on hers, she paused with a quizzical expression. Was this another of the prank gifts my family gave from time to time?

"Ron . . . ?"

"How do you like it?" No one could yet see what had once been a carrot.

"Well . . . " Sensing a possible catastrophe at my expense, my family hovered in. "What is that?" asked my sister. Moving to look in myself, I said, "It's a carrot pencil holder, you know, to go by a calendar or something." But then I looked in. Instead of a carrot in the box, there was this thing. I remember thinking some tiny animal must have crawled into the package, eaten the carrot, and then died itself, but it actually looked more like something that might have come *out* of an animal. Even the rubber band was indistinguishable. Suddenly, the full impact of my colossal screw-up was upon me.

"I guess it got rotten." I looked up into the faces of my family; they seemed to struggle momentarily to control themselves and then gave in, bursting into laughter. Kleenex was coming out, glasses were coming off, even my mother, who was one of those people who lose their breath when they get hysterical, was starting to make little high-pitched wheezing noises.

I didn't know where to look, and the tears finally came. My brother and sisters, however, were already scanning the remaining gifts for To/From tags with my name, making comments like, "I wonder if anyone else is getting a vegetable this year?"

Christmas Three

As Christmas morning, 2019, approaches, I wonder what makes these two memories surface. I should mention, although "The Christmas Carrot" story became a family favorite, the year after that disaster some strange things happened. Early in December, my oldest sister offered to take me shopping, when she normally acted as if she would die of embarrassment to be seen with me. My dad secretly advanced me a few weeks of my allowance, and my mom sat down with me one snowy afternoon to make a list of presents. Was this the same family who had delighted in my utter humiliation the year before?

My wife's gift of an unremarkable black helmet launched a twenty year odyssey of motorcycling, encompassing eight different bikes (the last five BMWs), legions of new friends, thousands of miles of adventure, and my penning of hundreds of features, reviews, and stories with riding at their core. Could my wife and kids have predicted where that helmet would take me?

It's funny how memories of a lifetime of Christmas mornings can blur and fade with time, but the seemingly unrelated helmet and carrot ones will forever be distinct. Maybe it's because they both taught me the same thing: the best gift you can ever receive is the love of your family.

Rain on the River Road

6

WHEN THE RAIN COMES . . .

One late afternoon about a week ago, my wife and I were returning from dropping off my grandkids when we rolled up behind a couple on a cherry red Gold Wing. I was in no rush to pass, since when I'm driving our car I like watching how another rider handles him or herself. They were just tooling along between fifty-five and sixty on the two lane, mainly staying in the left third in a steady track.

As our little convoy headed north, the skies dead ahead of us began to look darker and darker. If we continued in the same direction, it looked like we were all in for a real toad strangler. A few miles later, we crested a steep hill and were confronted by a band of thunderheads that stretched across the horizon, resembling a skirmish line of gigantic, puffy Abrams tanks, swelling in size and coloring into shades of dirty cobalt. Now I was really curious as to what the riders ahead of me would do. When we slowed for a one-stop-sign village, I told my wife, "Just watch; they'll pull in here under a convenience store awning or something." But the Gold Wing just continued on, accelerating out of the little town, back up to highway speed.

Both the pilot and his pillion had already wisely donned yellow rain suits, and they both had open face helmets with shields, but I'm not sure they expected the deluge that abruptly hit with a blast of wind and a wall of what seemed like fifty cent-sized rain drops. The Gold Wing slowed a tiny bit and glided to the right side of the lane, I guess in case someone like me wanted to pass, but I hung back, thinking the rear profile of my Subaru probably gave them more rear visibility than the bike's single tail light. The heavy Honda must have had good rubber, since it held steady through fierce winds and the rushing streams of water either rolling across or down the highway ruts and wear troughs in the pavement. The riders stayed clear of the center of the lane, where I figured they knew that's where they'd probably have the least traction.

Having been in a few situations like theirs myself, I had to admire that couple's pluck and their skill. A few years ago, I had impulsively chosen my 1150 R over my pickup for a three-hour run to a story interview, thinking I could slalom through the two bulging disturbances flanking my route on weather radar. It turned out the two storms merged into one torrential downpour, and I found myself creeping along, watching the road from what seemed like the back side of a waterfall. Water tunneled down through my "water-resistant" jacket into my crotch, prompting awkward explanations to everyone I met the rest of the day.

On another ride, this one down the legendary River Road tight along the Mississippi, the sky ripped open and hosed a buddy and me for hours. It had instantaneously turned what was supposed to be a carefree, scenic jaunt into a frantic battle with gulley washers running off the bluffs on one side while impatient drivers insisted on trying to dart around slowing semis on the other.

I often think riding through adverse conditions like these is an initiation, the cost of official admission into a guild of riders who've also been there, done that. But as James Lee Burke wrote in *The Neon Rain*, it may also be a kind of absolution. We have to pay our dues sometimes for the special privileges afforded to us as motorcyclists: the body buzzing exhilaration of pure acceleration, the euphoric illusion of being airborne over the highway, the occasional envious looks we get from those moored to four wheels, and the camaraderie of riders like ourselves.

I followed the Gold Wing for the next forty miles, until we finally broke out of the storm and pulled up two abreast at the first stop light in Eau Claire. The couple was talking animatedly on their intercom, I assumed about the ordeal they had just endured. Before the light changed and we would go our separate ways, I found myself wishing they'd look over my way, just for a moment, just so I could give them an approving nod and a hearty "thumbs up."

Blue Highways Moto-Cabin

7

A Place for Us

Recently I took what has come to be an annual jaunt down through the Driftless Area in southwestern Wisconsin. It's a trip I always look forward to, especially in late May, when the steep ridges and coulees carved out by countless spring creeks are carpeted in luscious shades of green, punctuated by the pink, white, and purple blossoms of apple, crab apple, and lilac.

After zigzagging in my own pokey way up and down Wildcat Mountain (now referred to as "The Tail of the Cow" by local riders), I stopped for an afternoon to visit with Brandy Vuich, who, with her husband Dan, has been operating the Blue Highway Motorcycle Lodge near Hillsboro, Wisconsin, since 2004. Sadly, I found out that Dan had passed in 2018 and that Brandy, realizing maintaining the lodge was too much work for one person, was in the process of selling this unique destination for riders.

Starting probably in the '30s, road maps color-coded those less-trafficked, more-twisted roads that motorcyclists covet in dark blue, hence the title of William Least Heat Moon's well-known book and the name the Vuiches gave to their lodge. Prior to moving to Wisconsin, Dan and Brandy had been avid riders, touring all over the Midwest and points beyond. Although both had good jobs, they had become disenchanted with suburban Chicago and had decided to seek a new life in the country.

"What we had was, we had a white board, and we wrote all the things we could do, living in the country—options—you could have a trout farm, or you could do this or that, and motorcycle B & B was one of those ideas," Brandy told me.

In their travels, they had stayed at motels and were often dissatisfied with the welcome they received and the accommodations. "Not to disparage little motels, but there were some that, well, we said, 'Let's prop the chair against the door knob 'cause this place is creepy.'" Brandy said that when they stayed at more upscale hotels, Dan would look out the window and laugh. "He'd say, 'Yeah, stay on the fourth floor and you can watch them load up your bike into the back of their van and you can yell: Hey, stop stealing my bike, I'll be down there in a minute!' We wanted a place where motorcyclists wouldn't feel out of place, and you're never going to be walking into a place where parents are going to be pulling their children closer 'cause there's a mo-tor-cy-clist walking in."

"We knew we didn't want to do food, so the idea evolved into having the cottages, and we began looking for land to do that. Neither one of us had any background with the hotel industry, never had worked in it at all," Brandy remembered. "We gave up everything, we sold everything . . . cashed in the 401Ks . . . the whole nine yards . . . We threw it all into this business. I'll tell you, we had no idea if it would make it. Our parents were like, 'A motorcycle lodge? Really?' Dan's brother said we'd have better luck with a bikini bike wash!"

Since it's such a mecca for riders, Dan and Brandy searched southwestern Wisconsin for a year and finally found a forty-acre plot on a ridgetop. Construction of the six cabins began in 2003, and although Dan did all the electric and plumbing, Amish craftsmen, who lived on adjacent properties, helped them build the six cabins and a shelter for groups. Despite the backwoods setting, Dan and Brandy were determined to make their cabins as welcoming and as mindful of the needs of road-weary riders as possible. All the cabins feature screen porches, galley kitchens, cycle ports, gas fireplaces, whirlpool baths, gas grills, and campfire rings. Special touches like boot dryers, motorcycle art on the walls, and the sound of a bike revving when you first turn on the lights make the cabins truly "rider-friendly." A network of paved paths almost too narrow for a four-wheeler and inaccessible to cars except in an emergency snakes into the woods and connects the cabins; in fact, a prominent sign at the office says, "No cars beyond this point."

Ever since I first heard of Blue Highway, I've searched and never found another destination for riders quite like it. True, there are more "Welcome Motorcyclists" signs on motel message billboards, and there are a few campgrounds, some with cabins, that principally serve riders, but I know of no other lodgings that only take guests traveling on two wheels.

Over the years, although Blue Highway became popular with all sorts of riders, Brandy says she and Dan never had any problems with guests. In fact, since many of the couples and groups staying at Blue Highway returned every summer, the lodge guestlist came to be more a list of old friends. "People calling to make reservations now, it's hard to get off the phone with them, like talking to a relative . . . we've built a family."

Blue Highway remains open this summer but only on weekends. Next year the new owners plan to keep the lodge the same, and it will be open every day, May through October. (For more information, visit bluehighwaymotorcyclelodge. net).

In a world of declining rider numbers and the continuing, sometimes negative, stigmas associated with motorcyclists, it's nice to know that places like Blue Highway Motor Lodge are still around. Riders are a special breed, and they deserve a few special places of their own.

Shameless Flirting

8

THAT GIRLFRIEND THING

For quite a few years now my wife has taken to describing whatever motorcycle I'm riding at the time as "your little girlfriend." Possibly born of jealousy (not likely) or of the fact that in French *motorcycle* ("la moto") is feminine (even less likely), my wife's demeaning attitude rankles me a bit, and I'm seriously considering putting her in her place with some serious eye rolling.

But not only is the "girlfriend" bit a little humiliating, it's an utter misnomer. With the risk of sounding politically correct, I feel the more accurate term for my bike would be "partner." I think of my ride as a collaborator—it starts, it runs reliably, and it offers an exhilarating perch on the way to our destination (if there even is one). In turn, I supply fuel, some skillful piloting (usually), and an admittedly dubious proficiency for navigation. It's actually more a contractual agreement than a romantic dalliance; dare I say, "friends with benefits"?

I must admit, though, as a teenager, romance did have something to do with my attraction to motorcycles. I was a firm believer then: girls dig guys with bikes. Now, as Valentine's Day looms and I fall into my annual reverie over past relationships, that myth has clearly been debunked, although often a motorcycle lurks somewhere in those memories.

My first Honda frequently could only be started by jumpstarting, unless there was a handy hill around. Jane Doe One (mysterious brown eyes, impious nature) would stand off to the side, looking away, as if waiting for a bus, refusing to acknowledge even knowing the sweaty guy huffing down the block until I had turned around and motored back to pick her up.

Jane Two (petite, curly red hair, and amazing freckles) wanted to learn to ride. After days of parking lots, she finally announced herself ready to pull out onto the highway. When a speeding Buick LeSabre suddenly bore down on us from behind, she seemed to suddenly forget everything she had learned about shifting, and the scream of the Honda Scrambler hitting its red line in first gear was only surmounted by my own voice shrieking, "SHIFT! SHIFT! PULL OVER! YOU'RE GOING TO KILL US! PULL OVER!!!" Either the near rear-end crash or Jane Two's discovery of my raging, hysteric response to a crisis was enough to end that experiment . . . in all respects.

After days of persuasion, Jane Three (Cranberry Festival Queen, clearly out of my league) finally agreed to let me take her to a concert for our first real date on my first real highway bike. Just as we reached the venue, a God-like voice boomed from an approaching police cruiser's speaker. "YOUR HEADLIGHT!" it said, and a quick check revealed mine wasn't working. The officer did an abrupt U-turn and pulled me over right in front of the queue of concert go-ers. I was so flustered—first date, out of my league, hundreds of gawking onlookers, seven foot cop—I completely blanked on how that bike's light only worked on bright and ended up sheepishly muscling the bike down to a parking lot. All I (and probably Jane Three) could do during the show was worry about how we were going to get home. Last date.

Later in college, I set my sights on a Jane Four, a coed from my Shakespeare class who was on crutches. After I rolled up to her apartment in my pretty much baffle-ess street bike for a visit, she informed me her broken leg was the result of a cycle accident. This apparently had more than dampened her zest for motorcycling . . . and inevitably, motorcyclists.

Through the vast cavalcade of women who've ridden on the back of my bikes (maybe five), I did develop the RPPP, "Ron's Potential Predictor for Passengers." Pillion holds on to the seat strap or side grips—probably going nowhere. Pillion clutches the sides of your riding jacket—hope springs eternal. Pillion locks arms around your midsection—Eight Ball says, "Looking good!" I've experienced all three variations, but as they say, your results may vary.

Any readers still with me might be thinking, "Yeah, but he did mention a wife in the beginning—someone had to like motorcyclists." Actually, my wife has never wanted to ride with me. *With me.* Returning home late from teaching a night class once, I saw Larry, a friend with a Gold Wing just pulling out of our driveway.

My wife, a little flushed, breathlessly said, "Larry gave me a ride on his motorcycle. That was fun."

"Wait a minute . . . WHAT???"

I guess it's possible there are women and men out there who can't resist the siren song of a dashing rider aboard a GS, or a GSX-R, or a Gilera, or a Street Glide. However, I've resigned myself to settling for motorcycling's less romantic, but still pretty alluring charms.

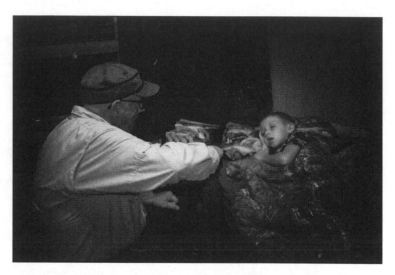

(With apologies to Alfred W. Miller)

9

UP AND OVER THE
GREAT DIVIDE

I awoke in my tent before sunrise to the chirps of chickadees and nuthatches that had been roused by the lightening eastern sky. No mattress, cot, or pad, the ground had been as soft as a feather bed, and my sound slumber had left me completely refreshed. I stirred the coals left over from last night's campfire, threw on some bone dry kindling for a quick, hot fire, and hung my pot of cowboy coffee over it to boil.

Though the morning was cool and wisps of fog clung in the pine boughs above me, my tent and bedding were dry. I hurried through rolling and strapping them to the GS's rack, impatient to hit the road. After filling my thermos, I warmed my hands on an enameled mug of joe and chomped on a handful of granola.

I took the time to slap together two sandwiches of elk sausage and provolone to tuck away for my summit, then zipped into my 'stich and thumbed the big bike to life. Bursting with the exhilaration of the clear, crisp morning and expectations for the ride that awaited me, I couldn't resist wheelying all the way out of the campground (to the consternation of a few early risers who had just emerged).

In a few moments, I was zigging and zagging up switchbacks. There was no one else on the road, and I pressed as hard as I wanted, skimming the foot pegs in the apexes. A dazzling slice of sun peeked over my shoulder, bathing the banks of aspens and parks of late summer grasses in warm shades of gold. Small families of deer and elk respectfully paused in the clearings, well away from the road.

The bike hummed on without complaint or hesitation as the air grew thinner and fresher, lightly scented with ponderosa pine, sage, and heather. Patches of snow soon flanked the road, but the tarmac was extraordinarily dry and grippy. The bike fell into the curves with no effort, often steering itself, and the miles fell away. My vigor and excitement grew with each step in elevation.

Finally, at a sign marking the continental divide, I parked, pulled out my sandwiches and coffee, and wandered out on a narrow precipice, where I sat on a cliff's edge. Barely after taking my first bite, I heard a deep "chuffing" behind me. It was a grizzly, nearly seven feet tall, advancing on his hind legs between me and the bike, his claws clacking on the rocks— escape was impossible. I had no option other than nervously offering one of my sandwiches in an outstretched hand. He cocked his head, then calmly accepted my proffer and joined me sitting on the rocky edge, both of us gazing into the shadowy valley below.

Bidding a farewell to the friendly bear, I began my descent down the west side, a glacier paralleling the road. Caution thrown to the crisp mountain breezes, I accelerated and plunged off a service road, landing on the glacier's hard-packed surface and roosting in a thin dusting of trackless powder. Like a downhill skier on a giant slalom course, I began carving my own Zs across the glacier's slope, pulling stoppies and letting the rear swing around at each change in direction.

At the bottom of the glacier it ramped up, and I flew off the whoop, only to land in a shallow runoff stream. As I cut down the middle, cutthroat trout immediately began leaping into the air all around me, and I reached back to open a side case and catch a few, along with buckets of icy water. Later, I would roll the fish in buckwheat flour and fry them in bacon grease alongside slabs of sourdough bread.

The stream grew into raging whitewater, and although still upright, I was helpless in its current as my crash bars caromed off boulders. Ahead I could hear the roar of a waterfall, and once again I accelerated to be flung off the drop-off, sail through the air, and land softly back on the pavement.

Ahead lay ten miles of gently descending sweepers, empty of any traffic. I dropped the bike into neutral, killed the engine, and as my speed increased, began brakelessly shredding the snake-like highway. All I could hear was the wind rushing over my windshield and past my helmet. Occasionally, cars would appear on the shoulders where the drivers had pulled over to safely text, check their emails, apply make-up, or admire the approaching motorcyclist.

When the road finally flattened out, I skidded into a wayside filled with a group of smiling riders who welcomed me before my sidestand was down. KTMs, Moto-Guzzis, BMWs, Ducatis, and even a few Aprilias were parked in a cluster circled by geared-up riders passing bags of oatmeal cookies, venison jerky, glazed donuts, and other treats. A woman with honey-blonde hair and yellow leathers passed out paper cups of fresh-squeezed orange juice.

After trading all of our stories and getting our fill of bike ogling, we all agreed it was time to fire up the bikes and make one more climb up and over the pass.

In the murky shadows of jagged-peaked mountains filled with grizzly bears, glaciers, cutthroat trout, and rushing mountain streams, a little boy with gold in his hair and cookie crumbs at the corners of his mouth snuggled down into his quilts. He murmured, "Good night, Grandpa. Thanks for telling me a story. That didn't really happen, did it?"

"Of course it did, Keegan." Shamelessly, I kissed his hair, turned down the light, and quietly closed his door.

A BMW "Lifestyle Accessory"

10

A "Lifestyle Accessory"

When March finally arrived in Wisconsin last year, along with the growing urge to get out on a motorcycle, I found a winter of binge-watching, junk food, and beer had done an excellent job of reducing me to a quivering ball of flab. I hadn't been a total slug, doing a little yoga to remain flexible and letting my lab, Penny, tow me around the block once a day, but as far as cardio, there was practically none.

I've been a bicyclist all my life and figured, as soon as the ice disappeared, doing a few miles each day on an old ten-speed would get me back to some semblance of fitness, at least enough to comfortably and safely use my motorcycle. But then a friend let me try his e-bike. Here was a novel way to get some exercise in a city of steep hills that was low impact (a blessing for my bad knees) and that I could adjust to my needs.

Obviously being a fan of the marquee, I first looked at BMW's e-bikes. Yes, BMW makes bicycles, with three models that offer pedal-assist motors. As you might expect, BMW bicycles are long on elegant design and quality components and have had good reviews, although of course, they're a little on the high side of comparable market pricing. They are currently marketed in the US through some BMW auto dealers as "Lifestyle Accessories," although you may find that's a surprise to salespersons.

No BMW auto dealers in my area handled bicycles, but a local bike shop was offering a deal on a popular model from Trek, which uses components similar to those of BMWs, so I pulled the trigger.

A little about e-bikes: The first thing to recognize is that most e-bikes aren't like scooters or motorcycles. The majority of e-bikes are "pedal-assist," which means you still have to burn some calories to get around, but a battery and a cunning little motor (barely visible on BMW models) can give you the boost you need to climb hills and extend your riding time. Is an e-bike "cheating"? I don't think so, at least no more than using a five-pound, carbon fiber, eighteen-speed with pencil-thin tires is cheating. Riding an e-bike in a mid-range boost setting versus a conventional bike has been compared to jogging versus brisk walking. Yes, riding an e-bike is still work, but most importantly, e-bikes enable decrepitude-battling people like me to become or continue to be bicycle riders. A couple of boomers I know who bought e-bikes said they literally giggle their way up hills.

And I'm not alone. Market research indicates e-bike sales rose over ninety percent in the last few years, and in the Netherlands, probably the most bike-happy country in the world, sales of e-bikes came close to surpassing those of conventional bikes last year. Wisconsin-based Trek claims e-bikes now make up more than a third of their sales and offers an e-version of practically every model they make.

Who's buying them? As you'd expect, e-bikes are popular with the forties plus segment, but who's buying e-bikes may be more a reflection of who has the most disposable income than who's just looking for a less taxing ride, since decent e-bike prices start around $1,500.

According to dealers I spoke with, in addition to commuters, more and more bicycle road racers are also using e-bikes for training because of their lower impact on knees and hips. He added that some bicyclists also buy e-bikes so they can keep up with a faster biking partner.

The increasing demand for e-bikes has, of course, spawned a bunch of brands, and price depends on the options you want and the style (mountain, street, cargo, folding, recumbent, trike, etc.) Many different brands use the same battery and motor, and distance before charging depends on which of usually four levels of boost (or none at all) you select. E-bikes typically can go thirty-five to a hundred miles without recharging. The most popular (and bike path legal) e-bikes assist up to 20 mph, so good brakes are essential, and a bit wider tire width is usually recommended. Class 2 e-bikes can have a throttle, which allows a rider to maintain a speed without pedaling and can go up to 28 mph; however, they are not legal on most bike paths.

One drawback to e-bikes is their weight. Because of the battery and motor, an e-bike can weigh fifty pounds or more, which not only means they're heavy to lift, but it also means a regular bike rack just won't do. I found a hitch mount rack I'm happy with for about $230.

Many riders will also want to "spring" for a better seat, since like motorcycles, most stock ones are typically poor, although BMW does claim its custom-designed Selle Royal saddles are exceptionally comfortable. Also, as with motorcycling, a good helmet is an essential accessory. To make my bike a grocery hauler I added a rear rack and a trunk. I'm now thinking saddle bags for an extended trip, maybe camping; with pedal-assist you can carry a lot of stuff!

As soon as weather permitted this spring, I charged my e-bike battery and set out to get my creaky body back into shape. At the time this column was due, Covid-19 had reared its ugly head, and I was conflicted about taking my motorcycle on longish trips and going in and out of rest stops, and while riding an e-bike is obviously no substitute for motorcycling, I felt confident I could cruise safely enough on my e-bike to be physically ready when I could again saddle up my Beemer without any qualms.

Zero Below Zero

11

THE LONG HELLO

I am writing this column in early May, 2020, so I have no idea what motorcycling (or the world) will look like when it is published in late June/early July. I only hope that the threats to our club's favorite mode of transport and to everyone's health have diminished.

I had disconnected the trickle charger and squeezed my GS out from behind the snowblower by late March and did a few shake-down cruises but not without feeling conflicted, since however remote the risks of riding, the hospitals around here were filled to capacity with Covid patients. I had to admit, motorcycling was not exactly "essential," and I finally parked the bike out of respect for my wife and kids' urgings. This year's "hello to riding" was going to be drawn out even longer than by that of the Frozen Tundra winter; however, on the upside, the sabbatical did give me

the opportunity to get some service done on the 310 GS
(Thank you BMW Motorcycles of Richfield for the curbside
pickup and delivery!) and the time to catch up on some
long-neglected reading.

One little book that caught my eye was *Zero Below Zero*,
a compilation of blog posts by Aerostich staffers about
an experiment they did in the winter of 2015-16. Zero
motorcycles had delivered one of their all-electric bikes to
the company headquarters in Duluth, Minnesota, to see if
everyday commuting with an all-electric bike was feasible
in one of the lower 48's coldest spots (Duluth ranks only
second to International Falls, Minnesota, for its record of
sub-freezing point days.) Although I commonly write for
owners of BMW motorcycles, the record of the Aerostich
riders' experiences makes for lively, interesting reading and
offers a new perspective on year-round commuting, not to
mention an intriguing harbinger of what lies ahead for all
motorcycle marques and all riders.

Apart from the weather considerations, I was especially
interested in what the riders thought about the transition
from gas-powered bikes to electric ones. Kyle Allen, an
Aerostich marketing and graphics co-worker, commented
that he felt not having to row through the gears and having
fewer variables to worry about made him more focused
on his surroundings and, as a result, a safer rider. Since
practically the only sound produced from the Zero was the
sizzle of the carbide studs on the pavement, other testers
also commented on how much more aware they were of
traffic around them. Riders also liked the finer throttle
control an electric motor offers, which helped keep the
Zero's back wheel from kicking out in slippery conditions.
(Duluth averages seventy inches of snow a year). In fact,
some of them said the Zero's 0-50 linear acceleration made
the temptation to slice and dice through traffic hard to
resist. Although it was conceded a bike like this Zero FX
was never going to be a tourer, as commuters, testers felt

electric motorcycles present an attractive option, especially since practically no maintenance is required. As Aerostich founder, Andy Goldfine, (a tester himself) wrote: "Electric vehicles sell us what all technology—from the beginning of everything—provides: Time."

Of course, how to adjust to Duluth's often sub-zero temps was a big question mark in this experiment, and the answers are food for thought for any rider seeking to stretch his or her riding season. Since the lithium-ion batteries in electric motorcycles have to stay warm to keep their charge, Aerostich designers came up with a custom-made heating blanket to plug in along with the charging cord (the bike was always left outside). Through trial and error, the riders found the best combinations for keeping themselves warm: heated bibs, riding suits, winter motorcycle gloves, winter boots, balaclavas, and a heated seat and grips. For traction, 150 carbide studs were screwed into tires that were purposely kept around 20 psi to increase their contact patch. For the most part, riders had few grip problems in Duluth's ever-changing conditions, although one tester reported the height of the Zero's seat made putting a foot down for stability on slippery pavement a challenge. Testers concluded after the experiment that commuting by motorcycle is reasonable through about seventy percent of a Duluth winter.

A year after the study, Zero asked Goldfine if he wanted another Zero to test, and he answered, "Heck no! My co-workers spent a lot of time with that Zero, instead of doing work... it is too much of a distraction!" (He added, however, that his co-workers mutinied when they learned of this, and they did get another one.) Electric motorcycles have enjoyed growing popularity and have made enormous advances since that 2015-'16 winter, with battery production costs falling, battery sizes shrinking, and horsepower and ranges increasing. Industry futurists predict that all motorcycle manufacturers will be offering electric cycles in the next six years, although prices will have to fall to make them more competitive with gas-burners. As the book notes, even electric flying motorcycles may no longer be the stuff of science fiction as corporate Goliaths like Google invest mountains of money on serious research and development projects.

The book *Zero Below Zero* is available at Aerostich.com for ten dollars or free on request with any product order.

12

OH, THE PLACES YOU'LL GO!
MOTORWAY MADNESS, PART ONE

Despite my love for gadgets, I've always steered away from mounting a little video camera on my helmet or to the front of the bike, although I've watched plenty of fascinating clips that others have captured. A bike camera just seems like one more thing I'd misplace, forget to charge, or helplessly watch tumble down the highway after I mounted it incorrectly. However, I had a little incident the other day that made me wish I had one going, since I saw a sight that I'm sure would have gone viral once I uploaded it to YouTube (assuming I could learn how to do that).

I was climbing a hill while riding the middle lane of three heading west. The speed limit was forty-five, which meant everyone was running sixty, and I was leading the squadron of cars that had jumped off at the green light at the bottom of the hill. Halfway up something big and black was crossing the highway. A bear? Nope, a big, mag-wheeled tire was lazily making loops across the lanes of traffic and back again. Apparently, the hill's incline and the camber of the pavement had set up just the right equation of pitch and angle to keep the tire rolling in almost perpetual circles.

At first, I figured the tire had bounced out of the old Chevy pickup slowing ahead in my lane, then I realized from the truck's tilt that one of the rear wheels had simply just broken off. It would have been hilarious if not for the stampeding herd of cars and trucks behind me that showed no sign of slowing down and beginning to weave across the three lanes, spraying to both shoulders. I got on the brakes for a moment, then visualized what the puny rear profile of my G 310 must look like; clearly this was a moment where acceleration would be my friend. I frantically tapped my rear brake as I slalomed between the rolling tire and the stalled pickup (there are no hazard lights on a 310) and blasted toward a clear space (well, as much as a 310 can "blast"). A quick glance at the stranded pickup showed its driver staring stolidly ahead, a man no longer with a plan.

Over the next couple days, I told everyone I met about my harrowing experience and was amazed to hear they all had their own astonishing stories of motorway madness. My neighbor, who had worked at a lumber yard, told me he had watched someone try to tie sixteen-foot two-by-fours TO THE BOTTOM OF HIS CAR. My son had passed a couple on the Interstate, each with an arm out holding a mattress that was levitating up off the top of their Corolla. One of my coffee buddies described watching one of those blue kiddie pools sailing over his car and out of sight—where it came from he had no idea. Another remembered sitting on his front step and watching a propane tank, one of those 250-pound yard pigs, bounce out of a utility truck and tumble into the ditch. Frost slowly spread over the tank as it hissed like a rhumba of rattlers; he dialed 911. My wife was once stopped at a green light next to a car full of young guys (pretty well lubricated, she guessed) trailering a fiberglass runabout. To the delight of his buddies, the driver punched it when the light changed, unfortunately jettisoning the boat off the trailer, the prop sparking into the tarmac.

A tool box cartwheeling down the road, a tower of hay bales tipping off a swaying wagon, tarps, life jackets, sheets of plywood, coolers, firewood, bags of garbage, bicycles, Styrofoam panels, there was no end to the stories, and I bet every one of my readers has another.

Every motorcycle book I've read that deals with safety stresses the need to be vigilant for all kinds of rubbish flying off vehicles, some suggesting paying as close attention to the vehicles you're following as you do the pavement, but maybe Dr. Suess said it best . . .

> *"Out there things can happen*
>
> *And frequently do*
>
> *To people as brainy*
>
> *And footsy as you"*

Or perhaps Serge Storms says it best when he cautions in a Tim Dorsey novel, "Be careful, it's dumb out there."

Dead Wheel in the Middle of the Road

13

"Oh, the Things You'll See!"

Motorway Madness, Part Two

In my previous column I dwelt on the frightening amount and head-scratching diversity of debris we riders encounter on the highway. Baby-head rocks, ruts, water crossings, and tree roots are obstacles we accept as coming with the territory off-road, but the terrifying drek we have to deal with on the pavement is often the result—let's face it—not of natural causes, but of cager negligence. In response to my column, quite a few readers had their own stories to share on the perils lurking on the highway, and here are a few . . .

For many years, I commuted across the Houston Ship Channel Bridge, a huge, six lane, metal-grate affair rising about 200 feet above the ship channel. The bridge has a long concrete approach then rises sharply to the top of the superstructure. There were no shoulders on the metal part of the bridge, just narrow emergency-stop lanes about half the width of a passenger vehicle. One morning I was cruising in the middle lane on the concrete approach at the usual 70-75 mph, when I realized I was seeing vehicles on the metal bridge darting for the emergency-stop lanes on both sides. Directly ahead of me, I could see what looked like a tall, dark brown, UPS delivery truck stalled in the middle lane, but it seemed to be getting bigger. Then it immediately came into focus: it was not a stalled delivery truck, it was one of those huge steel reels of undersea telephone cable, about twelve feet high, that had broken off the back of an AT&T truck and was now rolling backwards down the center lane toward me! I quickly peeled off for the left emergency-stop lane and had just stopped when the reel rolled by me at maybe 30 mph, whereupon it hit the side of the big blue garbage truck a few cars behind me. The garbage truck driver was, fortunately, uninjured, but the collision changed the course of the giant reel, which then took a sharp left, jumped the guard rail on the concrete bridge approach, flew down the embankment across a feeder road, then smashed into a small, vacant office building, which had a For Sale sign. The building was obliterated. It looked and sounded like a bomb going off! Being Houstonians, everyone looked around to see if there were any casualties, laughed with a shrug, and went on to work . . . (Dr. Brian S. Ziemer)

101 freeway in LA, northbound, 3PM as rush hour traffic starts to build. I'm in the fast lane on my R 1200 RT. Posted limit is sixty-five, so traffic is moving about eighty. I catch something in my peripheral vision and look to the right. A length of steel pipe about three feet long, which I later guessed to be part of scaffolding framework (I'm a contractor) plummeting earthward. Concrete K-rail on my left, cars fore, aft, and starboard. Can't accelerate, swerve, or brake. Pipe strikes center lane hard, ricochets directly towards me, and crosses my windscreen by millimeters. A few days later in my truck, traffic was stop-and-go in the same area, and I saw the pipe lying on the shoulder next to the K-rail. Had I been in the center lane or a mere second or two faster it would have struck me directly. Big sigh . . . (B. Curtis)

I live in the Central Valley of California. A common problem is "leaking livestock trailers." I doubt further explanation of the hazard is necessary . . . (Mike Crawford)

In my fifty years of riding I have avoided many (but not all) objects on the road. A particularly memorable time was when I was riding my Yamaha on a six-lane city street. As I was at the light, I noticed the Cadillac in front of me had one of those heavy duty screen doors tied to the roof with two pieces of twine. The light turned, and I attempted to move from the #3 lane to the #1 lane. Too late, the wind caught the screen and broke the twine. It pirouetted into the air and landed on my clutch lever. I stayed upright and just kept going . . . (Greg Barbre)

I was traveling US 19 North (also known as Killer 19) in the Clearwater, Florida, area, in the middle of three lanes with bumper to bumper vehicles following close enough to read my license plate. I was watching the car in front of me that had a ten-foot kayak on the roof. It broke loose and started spinning in the air (everyone was running about 60 mph), and all I could do was brace for the impact when it spun right around me and my trusty BMW K1200LT Hannigan trike. Vehicles behind and beside me were scattering and trading paint. I took the next turn off and started breathing again. (Mal Clingan)

One Sunday morning on the way to Palomar Mountain Observatory (San Diego) on Interstate 8, I came upon a mattress (queen size) in the middle lane ... (Bob Reil)

Riding my R90S (Daytona Orange, of course), I was gaining slowly on a small size dump truck as we were going slightly downhill on a four-lane undivided local highway. The truck's bed was filled across with twelve-foot, two by ten planks angled from the back of the bed to a projection about four feet over the cab, all in a row. As speed increased due to the downhill trajectory, liftoff velocity was achieved, and the pretty pink ribbon assigned to restrain the planks decided to end participation in the effort to restrain. All of the planks flipped out of the bed (as I flipped out inside my helmet), some landing flat and sliding, others landing on an end and taking big bounces in several directions. I somehow rode through this hazard and stopped to scream at the driver while throwing some planks back towards him. That incident really helped me focus on the crazy loads some people are carrying on their vehicles . . . (Paul Bates)

Another reader who responded to my column reminded me of the disquieting fact that may explain some of these near catastrophes: "Remember, half of the population has an IQ below the average." However, despite my hereditary bent toward cynicism, I'm hoping "this happened to me" stories like these may remind us to stay vigilant on the highway and may make our partners there take an extra minute to make sure that tie down is cinched, to think about what a seventy mile an hour wind can do to that garbage bag, or ponder the wisdom of disregarding how much a pothole can loft a loosely tied sofa!

2004 BMW R 1150 R

14

THE MOTORCYCLING LIFE, IN STAGES

After moving to northwestern Wisconsin a while ago, I was reunited with an old colleague from my teaching days. When we worked together thirty years ago, I knew Duey kept a crotch rocket in his little apartment's living room, but for some reason, we never really bonded over our love for bikes.

Anyway, when we got together again, this time at his new bachelor pad he had designed himself (half living quarters, half vehicle shop), I was stunned by the collection of bikes he had amassed. In the corner of his enormous, in-floor heated and immaculately-kept garage was a new Kawasaki Versys, and parked next to it was a military-looking Royal Enfield he used for poking around the country roads. Parked parallel were the Victory cruiser and the sleek-looking new mile-eater from Indian he used for trips out West. I should probably mention his gigantic garage also housed a Tesla and a Ford pickup. My mouth watered for the space he had created and also for his bikes, athough there were no Beemers (I will work on him).

When headed back home on my diminutive G 310 GS, the sun was taking its last peeks over the horizon, and it occurred to me Duey and I were in different stages when it came to what I'd call "The Motorcycle Life." But then I wondered, is there actually a progression of stages most riders go through?

I had in the back of my mind the distinguished research done by Dr. Robert Jackson of the University of Wisconsin-La Crosse. He had interviewed hundreds of hunters and anglers to determine if there was a consensus on general stages of development as they pursued their passions. The familiar adage *any fish, many fish, big fish, just fishin'* might describe many anglers' development, but his research revealed new and more detailed characterizations of the stages many hunters and fishers said they had experienced.

As I meandered my way back home, slaloming around deer, racoons, and other things that could go bump in the night, I replayed my own riding history and wondered how much it might reflect that of my readers. For instance, when I first got hooked on motorcycles as a teenager my longings had no boundaries—I'd ride anything I could afford (which wasn't much) no matter how unreliable or even dangerous, and I'd ride anywhere, dirt or asphalt. My "any fish" stage?

In college I became more pragmatic (although pragmatism was hardly my guiding principle then). I needed something half-way dependable and big enough to ferry me back and forth to school (and with any luck, carry an obliging passenger). It was the early '70s, and my buddies were all on Hondas, so I picked up a used CB350.

Then came another stage, which I suspect other riders have shared: a sabbatical. My wife and I had two children within two years, and our new situation had no room for what could be considered a luxury, and a dangerous one at that. Once my kids had grown up (at least in legal terms), I got a thumbs up from my wife. I had become even less of an "any fish/any ride" type rider, and (with a little more coin in my pocket) I fell for a used, but mint, BMW R65. Although kind of heavy for me and a little fraught with idiosyncrasies, I reveled in the classic machine and the appreciative looks I got from other serious riders.

I was back into the two-wheeled life, but also moving into another stage, this time in more of what Dr. Jackson might call a "How does it work?" period. I somehow had accumulated a little pack of Hondas: a CL360 Scrambler, a utilitarian CB250, and a 400 Hawk. All were nearly basket cases, but I had the naïve belief I could restore them. I also began to explore all the motorcycle literature out there, both on wrenching and riding skills. In the end (and after hours spent trying to rattle acorns out of mufflers), I had to accept that I would probably never have the patience to do restorations, but I did learn a lot both about bikes and about riding them smoothly (thank you, Mr. Hough).

Next, with eBay's help, I liquidated my little stable and took the Lake Express ferry across Lake Michigan to do a deal for what was to me the "big kahuna," a stunning Sienna Red BMW R 1150 R. Dr. Jackson might call this my "Trophy Stage." I loved that gorgeous bike, but after two years, I discovered how expensive final drives, integrated brakes, and clutch splines could be, and maybe foolishly anticipating what could happen next, I gravitated to a series of bullet-proof Suzuki V-Stroms. Of course, they weren't BMWs, but I liked their size and versatility, which then led me to a showroom deal on a F 700 GS.

The F7 was seemingly ideal, and I felt the ride I had chosen and the kind of riding I chose to do reflected a new-found freedom from peer pressure and the siren songs in magazine reviews; I was at a new stage where my age and experience were making my ride, well, my ride. The F7 was a great all-around bike and one I sorely miss, but with a skinny semi-retirement budget, a change in riding habits, and some physical limitations, I most recently downgraded to the

G 310 GS. Here again, this new stage of my motorcycling life jives with what Dr. Jackson calls the "Sportsman Stage." Instead of lusting for the "trophy," I'm now more focused on the whole experience, appreciating the pages from my past while at the same time the opportunity to still hop on a bike and dissect a few of the Driftless Area's serpentine two-laners. This new stage has me savoring camaraderie with like-minded others and even taking a stab now and then at mentoring younger folks.

As many outdoors writers discussing Dr. Jackson's theories point out, identifying shared stages of development doesn't mean those shoes fit everyone. Also, they're not necessarily linear; we can jump back and forth. In fact, sometimes when I'm on that little GS, I get that familiar rush from my first years, riding anything, riding anywhere, and enjoying the heck out of it!

15
ALL YOU'LL EVER NEED

The other day I was talking to my old riding buddy, Ralph, who had just sent me a book on trout fishing titled *Following in the Footsteps of Ernest Hemmingway* by Jay Thurston (Savpress.com). Ralph said, "Sometimes you find a book that is the only book you'll ever need." He was pretty much right about Thurston's book. But, I wondered, is there an "only book you'll ever need" when it comes to motorcycling? Looking at my bulging library of moto books, the answer is probably "It depends."

For instance, if you're looking for a comprehensive look at the history of BMW motorcycles, one book I'd recommend is Kevin Ash's *BMW Motorcycles: The Evolution of Excellence*. Ash traces the development of BMW motorcycles from 1917 up to about 2006, with interesting takes on historical influences, changing company philosophy, and marketing considerations. It's a small book in size, but it's packed with fascinating details and stunning photos courtesy of BMW Motorrad itself. A larger book published about ten years more recently is Ian Falloon's *The Complete Book of BMW Motorcycles: Every Model Since 1923.* Following the world-wide success of his first book, *The Ducati Story*, Falloon has written histories of many of the leading motorcycle marques, and this BMW tome covers every model from the R32 to the S 1000 RR.

If your need is for more of a comprehensive introduction to motorcycles and motorcycling, for me, the long-standing "bible" is David Hough's *Proficient Motorcycling (Editions I* and *II)*. I haven't yet found better books when it comes to making me a more confident and safer rider. Hough has taken some criticism for what some might consider sermonizing a bit, but his advice is backed up by data and extensive experience, and I have no objection to his taking safety so seriously.

Another book on the technical side I've endorsed in the past is Jim Ford's *The Art of Riding Smooth.* Jim has a talent for explaining in clear language subtle tweaks anyone can incorporate into their riding skillset. Warning: reading his book may leave you with an uncontrollable urge to ride what he calls the "invisible roads" of Appalachia or even reserve a spot in one of his Rider's Workshops.

Those looking for some entertaining trivia might want to pick up a copy of either or both volumes of Mark Gardiner's *Bathroom Book of Motorcycle Trivia.* Like most readers, I tend to forget about half of what I've read, or remember too much incorrectly, so find myself going back to these books (yes, often found in my bathroom), which feature 365 short pieces on all kinds of intriguing moto-facts, records, true stories, and events.

If you enjoy cozying up on long winter nights with narratives about motorcycling, of course I must pay homage to the guy I consider the god of moto-writing, Peter Egan. His *Leanings* books are compilations of columns that have appeared mainly in *Cycle World* since 1977, and for me, no other writing gets at the adventure that only motorcycling can provide in such compelling, conversational style. Returning to reread Egan's columns is like visiting old friends.

Although it's more difficult to nail down exactly why, I'd also recommend a book that, despite its 1998 publish date, continues to attract accolades. Melissa Holbrook Pierson's *The Perfect Vehicle* is both her personal story of her relationship with bikes and an objective examination of their place in our culture. Legendary moto-adventurer Ted Simon expressed my feelings about this book better than I can: "Bikers of all genders should read it to learn better why they do it. Many others will learn why they should."

This is nowhere near a complete list of books I would recommend to readers, just ones whose titles popped out from my bookcase as favorites and which I know are still available from major booksellers. Faced with long winter nights, a bike in the shop, or long waits in airport terminals, luckily there are many books out there in the moto niche which can, at least vicariously, embrace and enhance our passion for riding.

2019 BMW G 310 GS

16

First Anniversary: One Year with My G 310 GS

Whenever I switch bikes I always get a case of seller's remorse. Last summer, for really no other reasons than a change in my riding habits and my desire to try something new, I sold my BMW F 700 GS and picked up a 2019 G 310 GS. A glowing comparo between the 1250 GS and the newcomer 310 by Jocelin Snow in *Owners News* had piqued my curiosity, and a test ride and an appealing price tag (nicely discounted by my MOA membership) sealed the deal.

Make no mistake, that F7 was a great bike with some outstanding features, but, well, as I've mentioned here before, I have kind of a disease when it comes to changing vehicles (currently on my fifth BMW). After a year of ownership (though only a thousand miles—thanks, Covid), I'd like to offer my impressions on the bike called, somewhat derisively, the "Baby GS."

First off, from when it was introduced in 2017, I was attracted to the 310's looks, and my bike regularly gets compliments. It really doesn't look like an entry level motorcycle, and the "beak" and the tank shroud echo its bigger siblings' iconic lines.

The ergonomics work for me, too. At 5'9", the reach to the bars and pegs fits me well, and I can almost flat foot at stops. However, when I stand up on the pegs, the reach to the bars and use of the rear brake pedal are both awkward (more about accessorizing later). Although I've always found OEM BMW saddles better in the showroom than on the road, the 310 is really quite comfortable—a hundred-mile sit is not a problem. Being the lightest BMW (375 lbs.) also makes horsing the bike around in the garage and wrangling it in the dirt much easier than with a bigger bike. Although it's not really an ergonomic issue, I've found the sidestand to be a little too tall; special care has to be taken when parking.

Adjusting to the little GS's power band was a challenge at first. There was a lot of rowing through the six gears, as one might expect with a 313cc motor, and the single's appetite for soaring rpms takes some getting used to. Paul Glaves, a long-standing *BMW Owners News* contributor and BMW savant, and his wife, Voni, (more miles on a bike than I can imagine) both have 310s, and Paul recommends a shift/mph pattern that exploits the bike's power above 6,000 rpm: "First [gear]—quite slow, 2nd good for 10 to 35 mph, 3rd from 20 to 50 or 55, 4th up to about 70, 5th to over 80, 6th and 5th about the same top speed between 85 and 90. In 5th you hit the rev limiter, and in 6th wind resistance overcomes horsepower." The bike has no problem with legal highway speeds, but of course, passing requires some planning.

Since it's a thumper, the baby Beemer is prone to vibration. I've been told that vibration decreases as the engine "beds in," but I'm skeptical. The mirrors on my 310 are terrible on the highway (more to come on add-ons), and all 310s seem to have a problem with a headlight that jiggles on its mount with every little bump, although ADV forums are rich with DIY hacks for both problems, and I plan to try some. Suspension I'd rate as fair to good, depending on where you're riding, and the tool needed for adjusting the rear takes me back to my Honda days.

The Farkle Factor: One of the BMW G 310 GS's keys to its phenomenal sales figures is, of course, it's price, and without spending anything on upgrades, it's shown itself to be an inexpensive, reliable, and spirited commuter and a fun off-road weekender. But for those, like me, who can't resist farkling, there are a few improvements I've made. Luggage: I added a Pelican case knock-off for a top box, which works fine without adding much to the bike's crosswind profile. (It doesn't like a lot of wind, but it's no worse than the two V-Stroms I've owned.) I also found some nifty Nelson-Rigg Dual Sport Saddle Bags (nelsonrigg.com) that expand to carry twenty-four liters of stuff without getting too close to the muffler. A Givi windshield with a cheap spoiler zeroed buffeting, and to knock down vibration and tingling hands, I added a heavy handlebar strut, Original Grip Buddies (originalbeemerbuddies.com), and a rubber bushing for the handlebar clamp. I still get some tingling, but reminding myself to hold the grips like a potato chip or a toothpaste tube (as experts recommend) helps.

I love the set of SRC Moto crash bars I added (July 2020 *ON*) and also the Cyclops Signal Inserts that make the bike much more conspicuous (April 2020 *ON*). Lower-cost mods include a sidestand foot, a CrampBuster, and a voltage monitor. Apparently, there was an alternator issue with the 2018s, but I have seen no hiccups in the charging level on my 2019. A size large Tool Tube (thetooltube.com) for an air compressor sits under my rear rack.

Still to come: The oil filter on a 310 hangs right out there on the front of the motor, and the plastic skid plate is more cosmetic than functional, so that's got to be dealt with. Also, many 310 GS and R owners seem to like upgrading to an aftermarket silencer, but I'm okay with stock. As I mentioned, a footpeg mod for off-road would be nice, as would maybe some Rox risers (roxspeedfx.com)—Paul recommends two-inchers. A primo set of handguards like ADV Guards from MachineArtMoto (machineartmoto.com) is probably in the cards; they're the best I've seen, and I know from previous experience they have an added benefit of damping vibration. For the mirror problem, I'm lusting after some Mirrorloks (motomanufacturing.com/mirrorlok).

Apart from a brake caliper recall and replacement, I've had no mechanical issues with the 2019 BMW G 310 GS (although the brakes curiously felt a little spongier after change-out).

After a year of riding, I'd say its diminutive size, no-frills design, low price, and frisky handling rekindle a lot of the appeal that first gave me the motorcycle bug.

TFT for the "Perfect Motorcycle"

17

THE PERFECT MOTORCYCLE

I think I've owned almost twenty different bikes, usually just one at a time. There was nothing really wrong with any of those motorcycles that made me want to sell or trade them in for something different, but my inherited compulsion to try "the next thing" is just too strong, stronger than the hassles of advertising, haggling, paperwork, taxes, etc. On the other hand, none of those bikes was perfect. As I plod toward that time when I contemplate what may be my last motorcycle, I have to wonder, "What would be a perfect bike?"

Well, first of all, the perfect bike would obviously have to be red. Not "Brandywine," "Persian Rose," or "Cranberry Sunrise"—just plain old fire engine red. Red is passion; red is energy; red is danger; red is the color of fast. Also, red was the color of my very first motorcycle jacket. I know black has always been a pretty popular color for a bike, and although black is badass for sure, it gives a brooding, sinister look that's just not me.

Weight would then be a fundamental consideration for a perfect bike. It should be heavy enough to hold its own on the Interstate and in fierce crosswinds, but like a Great Lakes freighter that sheds its ballast to take on more cargo, the perfect bike would have the capacity to drop a couple hundred pounds as it rolls into the garage. A card-carrying member of the BBOA (Bad Back Owners of America), I hate heaving a big bike around in the garage to make room for all the other ephemera I've accumulated. I can't count how many reviews I've read of two-wheeled behemoths that approach the weight of a Mini Cooper where the writer meekly says something like, "Once underway, the bike becomes very maneuverable."

Related to weight considerations, there'd be no worries over picking up the ultimate two-wheeler when it was shiny side down. I'm envisioning hydraulic arms that would extend from either side of a dumped bike to jack it up to vertical. The arms would then retract and disappear, preserving the rider's image of rugged self-reliance.

Height would be another consideration for a perfect bike. Enough clearance to clear baby-head rocks would be required, but the bike would stoop to Harley saddle heights for mounting/dismounting or stopping at lights. I suppose you could even wiggle the air suspension switch at stop lights just to see the wide-eyed expression of astonished cagers as you pogo up and down.

The perfect motorbike would also be the pinnacle of safety. In addition to 360-degree air bag protection, the motorcycle would automatically deploy four small rockets from its undercarriage to leapfrog the bike over zombie drivers mindlessly turning left in front of me. This feature could also include a "Hover Mode," handy when drivers coming from the right on roundabouts can't seem to comprehend the meaning of "yield to vehicles approaching from the left." Hover Mode would also deploy when sensors detected a danger of being rear-ended by a driver eating, texting, checking their GPS, talking on the phone, lighting a cigarette, etc.

Deer and other varmints could be temporarily frozen at the roadside with a perfect bike's SSR (Super Stun Ray). And dogs giving chase would be turned away with a blast of chaff consisting of smelly sausages, chicken bones, and three-day-old walleye guts.

Is your best "battered baby seal look" not garnering its usual allure from innocent bystanders? Totally frivolous, but still probably a popular option for a perfect motorcycle would be a facial cloaking device. With it, the riders could shed their usual humdrum visage and transform it to that of George Clooney, Scarlett Johansson, or any other stunning Hollywood icon (selectable on the TFT display of course).

Tires with unlimited mileage, bottomless gas tanks, spa-massage saddles, adaptive cruise control, indefinitely robust oil and brake fluid, and heads-up displays would all be options for the ideal road steed, but then again, one has to ask, is "perfect" really what we're after?

Isn't accepting the exposure to the elements, the physical discomforts, the self-induced solitude, and the inexorable demand to "live in the moment" what separates us from those pitiable beings on four wheels? Couple that with the exclusive opportunities motorcycling offers for adventure, independence, camaraderie, and a singular sensation akin to flying, and well, as *30 Rock's* Tina Fey once wrote, "Perfect is overrated."

I Fool a Fish

18
"The Opener"

Starting when I was a kid, opening day of trout fishing always held a special kind of nervous anticipation for me. The nights during the week before the May opener usually found me scouring the First English Lutheran Church's lawn for night crawlers, the afternoons spent sorting out my gear, and it was tough getting any sleep on Friday, checking the alarm clock every hour to make sure I would be fidgeting on a stream bank before dawn. As I've gotten older my eagerness for the opening has ebbed. Now I prefer to leave the first weekend to the angler invasion, waiting until later, when I can get a quiet stretch of creek to myself.

My attitude toward the first motorcycle ride of the season, in a way, mirrors my fishing history, in that I used to obsess about the weather and count the days until I could slide in the battery and blow out the cobwebs from too much time spent out of a saddle. This year, I did venture out in what Wisconsin-ites call "Fool's Spring," a few days in March that hit the 60s, but the amount of salt and sand still on the roads and the seeming obliviousness of cagers who hadn't had to look for motorcyclists in a while led me back to the garage to wait until April. Like my more casual approach to another fishing season, my first real days of riding don't generate the "fire in the belly" the way they used to.

I'm not sure if it's a good thing or not, but I find myself much more tentative than I used to be on a bike, especially on those first few forays. I avoid the city as much as I can and seek out the wiggly Driftless Area county trunks and town roads that Wisconsin riders are so lucky to have. I take it easy on the bike's mechanicals until I feel confident everything's working right and keep the speed down as I reach into muscle memory that's been idle for five or six months. As with the initial fishing outings, where I have to sharpen my focus on the "now" to catch a few trout, on the bike I have to break away from the lackadaisical attitude I have as a car driver and remember that piloting a motorcycle is a whole different process, as demanding as it can be rewarding. Incidentally, recent research by neuro-scientists suggests all-consuming activities like riding and even fishing, which they say require "embodied cognition," generate dopamine and endogenous opioids, pleasure center stuff, but we all knew that, didn't we?

In the last couple of years, I've tried to set goals in the spring for improving my riding skills, last year experimenting with pre-positioning body position and posture—"kissing the mirrors" ala Jon DelVecchio—in an effort to skewer corners with more composure and elegance. This year, I'm working on my tight turning. The closest I've come to dumping the bike has often come about by trying to duck walk through U-turns and losing my footing. So, I've been watching videos, reading, and turning figure-eights in deserted parking lots in preparation for that moment that I'm sure is coming: lost on a steeply cambered, country two-lane and forced to turn around, in the dark, in the rain. I work on looking through the turn, thinking about pressure on the pegs, keeping the revs up, and feathering the clutch. Making tight turns has never been something I've been comfortable with, but I'm positive, as Vince Lombardi once said, "Practice does not make perfect. Perfect practice makes perfect."

On those first rides, I'm not only resurrecting muscle memory but also neuron memories of ways to avoid getting hit. With an oncoming car signaling a left turn, I think about escape routes and cover the brakes. At intersections I look both ways, even when I clearly have the right of way, which, as we all know, means little when you're in a face-off with a minivan. Running abreast with drivers on their phones while holding a dog and coffee cup, I either accelerate or fade back. I tap the brake and waggle when slowing for lights or stop signs, and I try to focus on the front wheels of vehicles waiting to pull out into traffic—I've found watching drivers' faces can often be no indication of whether they see me or not. All of my Subaru's safety features, like proximity warnings and automatic braking, have made me lazy, and now I have to revisit old habits like avoiding blind spots, allowing for safe following distances, and staying out of the middle of my lane.

All of this doesn't exactly enhance the anticipation, excitement, and adventure of riding again; however, I have a feeling a little prudence will probably pay off all riding season long.

Rake

Trail

19

How Smart Is You?

It never fails. At least once a year I catch a news story about the appalling state of intelligence of Americans. You know that song: a survey reveals high school seniors can't tell you in which war America won its independence, some college grads name Opra Winfrey as our vice president, etc. In fact, when people on the street were asked "Are you stupid?" by talk show host Jimmy Kimmel, half replied, "Yes."

Are we getting dumber? Maybe, but I can't say I'm any paragon of wisdom myself (and advancing age hasn't helped). However, at least BMW motorcycling should be something we enthusiasts know about, right?

Maybe this basic quiz will reveal the depth and breadth of your cycle knowledge (answers at the end):

1. A red "ABS" light on your dash indicates . . .
   a. You need to find a sticker to cover it.
   b. It's time to start doing crunches again.
   c. Your local BMW service shop has a cash-flow issue.
   d. Anti-lock brakes are working (or maybe not!)

2. "Rake and Trail" refer to . . .
   a. A great subject for ending any conversation with a non-rider.
   b. Mathematical algorithm requiring a working knowledge of the Schrodinger Equation and the Fourier Transform.
   c. Two dimensions your bike desperately needs, but you didn't know it had.
   d. Something possibly made up by Jack Riepe (who's also rumored to be the source of the phrase *crotch rocket*).

3. The abbreviation "Nm" stands for . . .
   a. No Motorcycles Allowed.
   b. Newton meter.
   c. "Nice move, Knievel" (usually uttered by a friend after you drop your bike).
   d. Nothing much.

4. As a motorcyclist encountering fresh cut grass in the roadway, you should probably . . .
   a. Stop, dismount, and give the guy on the riding lawn mower a stern lecture (with PowerPoint) on "Kinetic Friction Force."
   b. Stop, take a photo and make a snarky Facebook post.
   c. Turn around, go home, get leaf blower.
   d. Go around it.

5. Complete this phrase: "Loud pipes . . .
   a. . . . make your neighbors stop talking to you."
   b. . . . create a convenient method for contributing to your city's general fund."
   c. . . . say 'I have a loud motorcycle (and you don't).'"
   d. . . . for some reason, cost more than quieter stock ones."

6. As you approach a roundabout, you should . . .
   a. Make an immediate U-turn, since only one out of ten US motorists really understands the rules.
   b. Proceed with caution.
   c. Hold down your horn button, scream as loud as possible, flash brights, wave arm.
   d. Pause to check your insurance coverage.

7. Rider etiquette demands that, when approaching another oncoming rider on the highway, you should . . .
   a. Point two fingers at the ground with left hand.
   b. Offer a desultory nod.
   c. Ignore any motorcycle other than a BMW.
   d. Pull over to discuss oil preferences.

8. The best line to use with your significant other when you want to buy a second motorcycle would be . . .
   a. "It's good for the economy."
   b. "It's for you."
   c. "I'll be gone a lot more."
   d. "I can always sell it for a profit."

9. "BMW" stands for . . .
   a. Bayerische Motoren Werke.
   b. Bavarian Motor Wheels.
   c. Bavarian Marriage Wrecker.
   d. Befestigungsanlage Maximalgeschwindigkeit Wacholderbranntwein

10. What is the current slogan for BMW motorcycles?
    a. "Make life a lifetime."
    b. "Make life a ride."
    c. "Get a life and ride."
    d. "Ride like you like life."

11. The BMW logo was inspired by . . .
    a. A spinning propeller.
    b. An extremely elementary version of checkers.
    c. The flag of a German state.
    d. A story problem involving one quarter the area
       of a circle from an eighth-grade geometry text.

Answers:

   1.   (d.) Seeing that light at start-up is always good for instilling a few moments of dread, though.

   2.   (c.) And without both you'll find cornering much more exciting!

   3.   (b.) Incidentally, mentioning that 1 Nm is equivalent to 0.738 lbs./ft. is yet another way to end any social conversation.

   4.   (d.) But you should know that "c. wet leaves" is the answer to the question #7 on the Wisconsin DMV's Motorcycle Endorsement Test (25 multiple choice questions, 45 min. time limit)

   5.   (d.) But don't be surprised if your neighbors start shooting their grass clippings into your driveway.

   6.   (b.) If you want to continue making "life a ride," yield to vehicles approaching from the left, otherwise do not stop!

   7.   All. But I prefer "the queen's wave."

   8.   Not sure, but do let me know if any of these work.

   9.   I'd guess (a.), but I prefer "Bring More Weinerschnitzel."

   10.   (b.)

   11.   (c.) Yes, BMW did make airplane engines, and yes, it looks like it could be a spinning propeller, but, get over it, it's derived from the Bavarian flag colors. End of discussion!

For a more reliable BMW motorcycle quiz, visit zeroto60times.com/quiz/bmw-motorcycle-quiz/

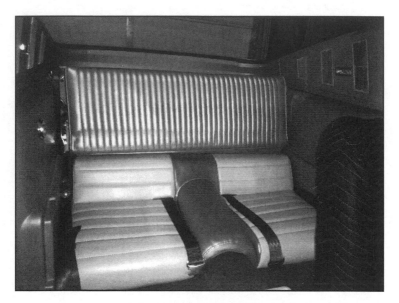

The Torture Chamber
(Otherwise Known as the Backseat of a '64 Mustang)

20
MY FAVORITE MISTAKE

One February when I was in college one of my friends got the brilliant idea of going to Mardi Gras for the weekend. That doesn't sound unreasonable, until you know we went to college in Eau Claire, Wisconsin, 1,200 miles from New Orleans. Five of us immediately hailed the idea as having the makings of a grand adventure, despite the fact that the only available car was an aging 1964 Ford Mustang: two bucket seats and sardine-like seating for three in the back, with the middle position sporting maybe a half-inch of foam padding over the driveshaft hump. Hey, we were children of the '60s.

We left early on a Friday morning, and within the first ten miles, it was obvious that sitting on the middle of the back seat was a torture capable of breaking the strongest-willed secret agent. After much debate, a rotation order and short list of rules were agreed to. Driving shifts were limited to 125 miles or two hours, whichever came first (clock and odometer were watched scrupulously); however, if a driver made a "mistake," he had to give up his seat. At first, "mistakes" could mean gross errors like falling asleep, getting a speeding ticket, having a near collision, or wandering off the highway, but as the miles piled up and derrieres were more bruised and battered, the definition and scope of what constituted a "mistake" grew exponentially.

Probably none of us suffered more in that cramped back seat than Ralph, my lanky 6'3" roommate, a guy who was about as easy-going as you can get. Despite his size (actually ill-suited to riding anywhere in that Mustang), his gentle, apologetic nature made him easy prey for the rest of us when he took the driver's seat. We all leaned forward and keenly watched him like four turkey vultures, praying for the slightest error, and it usually didn't take long before he was voted out—a lane change without signaling, failing to make a complete stop at a stop sign, or exceeding the speed limit by a mile per hour or two. Poor Ralph.

Suffice to say, my one wide-eyed and open-mouthed evening at Mardi Gras and a few hours of sleep on a greasy motel room floor wasn't too grand of an adventure; however, the idea of making mistakes has been on my mind lately whenever I head out on a motorcycle. I've begun playing a little game with myself, counting my mistakes, ever striving for "the perfect ride." I like to think I make fewer errors and ones of lesser consequence as I've grown older and gained experience and knowledge, but, you know, unlike wine, becoming a "vintage" rider doesn't necessarily mean becoming a better one. Forgetting to cancel a directional (currently on an old bike), starting in the wrong gear (again, old bike), changing lanes without doing a head-check, stretching the safe boundaries of a curve, suddenly realizing I'm twenty miles over the speed limit, hitting a pothole that could have been avoided . . . I'm sure you get the idea. I've made them all (and more) at one time or another.

On a ride in the city the other day I paused at a red light, ready to make a right turn. A UPS truck was approaching on a cross street from my left but was signaling a right turn. As I eased out the clutch and entered the roadway, a little red Kia going straight magically appeared from behind the truck. My only option was to pull over next to the curb to avoid getting side-swiped. That mistake was all me; hopes of a perfect ride dashed once more.

And yesterday, while waiting at a light, I noticed a purple Dodge Challenger in my rear-view mirror coming up behind me and running way too hot. Instead of looking for an escape route or manically pumping my brake light, I just watched the cager bear down on me, finally chirping into a skid a few feet short of my license plate. When the light changed the driver blasted past me, without so much as a remorseful glance my way. I wonder if he's counting his mistakes?

In *King Lear*, Shakespeare wrote "striving to better, oft we mar what's well," and rest assured I'm not going to let counting mistakes and worrying about a "perfect ride" get in the way of enjoying a good romp on a bike. However, at the same time, of all the mistakes I may make, probably the biggest is fooling myself into believing I don't make them.

Not Yours!

21
SHOP TALK

When the snow's deep outside and thoughts of skimming down the highway are a fantasy, I can't resist the impulse to tinker with my bike a little. *Tinker* is a pretty appropriate verb choice for my garage exploits, certainly more fitting than *service*, although my wife would probably choose *putz*.

I do have a bigger garage than I used to have, although it's not heated and I have a few more tools that I've accumulated over the years, I'm still about as shy on expertise as I often am on patience, so any of my mods or maintenance, by most rider's standards, are pretty elementary. Then again, what else can you do when the weather man's talking about a wind chill that "feels like" you'll never see temps in the zero plus column again?

Usually, it seems like the prep work for a day in my "shop" takes the most time. First, I have to clear my workspace of our mainstay Subaru and my Jurassic Period Ford Ranger. The fit is so tight between the two vehicles that the car has to come out first, before I can even open the door to the Ranger, and then backing that out is a white-knuckle operation, since the truck's body work is held together by a rusty thread threatening to snag and drag along garden hoses, the odd bicycle, or my Beemer itself.

Next, I grab the push broom and, with a misguided impulse toward tidiness, turn the road sand, melting slush, Ranger oil, leaves, and mouse droppings into a more evenly spread slurry over the garage floor—I know I'll invariably be rolling in it no matter what kind of bike surgery I'm doing. This is followed by a quick inventory of tools. It's quick, because my tool collection is pretty meager: old open-end wrenches (some that have obviously done service as ball peen hammers), a Sears socket set (two or three sizes currently AWOL), and a headband light with dead batteries augmented by one of those yellow, six million lumens worklights—look directly into it and you'll be seeing spots all day long.

After the customary appraisal, it's off to borrow my friendly neighbor's fancy-pants digital torque wrench, where I try to contain my boiling jealousy for his HEATED, ANTI-FATIGUE INTERLOCKING FLOOR MAT-ED, FLOURESCENT LIGHTED, WALL-MOUNT TV-ED SHOP SPACE. (There's even a winch on the ceiling, for crying out loud.) My other neighbor has my air compressor, since he's young and he and his wife are slowly demolishing and rebuilding their house, I surmise, from the inside out.

I have an old dog bed that seems free enough of varmints to lie on, and I pull on a ratty deer hunting jump suit to stave off the cold and floor muck. The day's project goals include installing a centerstand, new mirror stalks, and handguards and flirting with the prospect of an oil change. However, between breaks for coffee, fussing with tuning the wandering radio dial to NPR, cursing the dog for licking my face at critical moments or grabbing the printed instructions, helping my wife sort out her Zoom meeting glitch, more coffee and subsequent pee trips, eternities spent on the floor looking for a dropped spacer (which will inevitably lead to a half-hour spent pawing through the fastener bins at the hardware store), answering an infuriating robo call about my expiring car warranty, and of course, the critically important nap, well, I'll be lucky to get the mirrors on.

Anyway, somehow at least one thing gets done, and the whole process has to be reversed. Wrench and compressor back to neighbors, what tools that can still be found stowed, bike back on the track stand and shimmied into a corner. As the winter gloom descends outside and a few, tentative flakes begin to sift down, the vehicles have to be sandwiched back into their stalls.

This, then, is a moment that must be set aside for cracking a Leine's and surveying once again what Ron, master of his universe, hath wrought. Time for a frosty swig, a self-satisfied sigh—order restored over chaos, man once more triumphant over machine. And with a last glance to the arena of my day's conquest and a turn toward the cozy kitchen's door, there it is on the floor, the damned missing spacer, glaring up at me, seeming to say, "What a Putz!"

Pay No Attention to the Brand of this Bike.

22

Tip-Toeing Off the
Reservation

Warning: The following column focuses on a motorcycle that is not a BMW. Yes, I know, HERESY!

This past spring, I succumbed to the disease I've mentioned here before, the inherited compulsion to buy a different vehicle, in this case a motorcycle, about every two years. I've been riding a carousel of large and small, new and old BMWs for the past twenty years and am a shameless disciple of Bayerische Motoren Werke, but hey, sometimes you have to mix it up a bit, and in an impulsive disregard for my savings account and an eye roll from my wife, I picked up a 2014 Honda NC700X.

I had long been curious about the Honda NC7, because, well, it's a curious bike. Two main characteristics of this bike have made it kind of an oddball in Honda's line, in fact in that of most motorcycle manufacturers. One, its gas tank is under the seat. My 2016 BMW F 700 GS had the same feature (no longer true on the most recent model) and may have even been inspired by the Honda, although BMW had handled it in a much more elegant way, putting the fill cap just below the side of the saddle, while the Honda requires you to lift the seat to refuel. I'm a fan of that tank position because, together with its long-stroke pistons lying down at a 62-degree angle, the NC has a low center of gravity, thereby making it, in my mind, more maneuverable, both on the road and in the garage.

Secondly, and I think Honda's alone on this one, the NC700 has a "frunk." Where a gas tank would normally sit, the Honda has a hatch covering a storage compartment large enough to hide a full-face helmet. Even if you don't use it for a helmet nest, it's pretty darn handy, making a tank bag seem superfluous, and behind a little door in the compartment, the battery is very accessible, not exactly a common trait on some Beemers. Speaking of electrics, my new-to-me 2014 NC700X has a fairly primitive electrical scheme, not the CAN Bus I've worked around on my BMWs when adding accessories.

Reminiscent of the R 1150 R I rode all over for two years, the Honda has an amazingly broad torque curve, with ninety-five percent of the peak power at a measly 2,800 rpm. The bike is delighted to tool along in sixth gear up and down the highway at 3-4,000 rpm, and basically you can ride it around town all day hardly leaving second gear. This power setup, along with some pretty nifty engineering, also partly explains why the fuel-injected NC700's powerplant gets over 70 mpg, although admittedly, you're not going to be blowing the doors off some comparably-sized bikes at the stop lights.

The Honda rarely raises an eyebrow at BMW meets, since its fat, two-into-one exhaust can, mini beak, and flowing design lines make it resemble those of a BMW, and maybe also because the bike is a little rare in the States and more popular in Europe. In my home city of 70,000, I've only seen one other sister ship, and I know the owner, who also rides a vintage Bonny and a new Africa Twin. Probably one key to its popularity in Europe as a courier bike is the "DCT" variant of the NC700 that, perish the thought, has an automatic transmission. I'm not sure the Honda NC7 garners the respect a GS, R, or K bike does in a parking lot, but it does generate walk-overs by other riders who, like me, are . . . curious.

Of course, for its lower price, this aged Honda does have some shortcomings. Like the BMW Funduro I once owned (and kind of regret selling), you tend to slide forward on the OEM seat as you ride, which can get uncomfortable in your swimsuit area. That fuel cap under the seat thing is also a pain when you have gear strapped over the pillion area. And although the 2021 NC700X has some great upgrades, my 2014 lacks a bunch of things I appreciated on the BMW F 700 (now grown to a 750, just like the newest Honda): ABS, self-cancelling directionals, tire pressure monitors, stainless brake lines, and a choice of ride modes (the 2021 Honda has selectable ride modes and ABS). Unlike the GS, the only suspension adjustment on my Honda requires cranking the preload spring collar (not a simple task). The 2014 also uses Phillips head bolts in spots, as opposed to much more robust Torx and Allen heads found on Beemers. Honda's NC700X has been called an "adventure" and a "dual-sport" bike, although with its smaller, wider wheels and street tires in stock form, I think any adventures would best be limited to pavement.

As for longevity, after 62,000 miles, one NC700X owner wrote this bike has proved to be "less a bike, more of an investment!" Have I gone off the reservation forever? Not likely. In my haste to fulfil all my motorcycle fantasies before I'm too decrepit to ride, I'm still browsing for a gently used

RT, a bike I've always wanted to take on an extended trip. I guess now you could call me an occasional outlier; however, as a quick gander down the row of bikes at any rally will tell you, despite some of the snarky comments you might see on Facebook, I've always found the motorcycle community to be a pretty big tent, ready to accept anyone who shares a passion for riding, no matter what kind of bike they ride.

Morning in "The Wilderness"

23

ROUGHING IT?

One of the reasons I bought a bigger bike last spring was I thought I might, after a long sabbatical, like to try moto-camping again. But I had to wonder, could a bike hold all the stuff these aging bones would require to rough it for a night or two at a fairly spartan campground? And would the prospect of pump-it-yourself water, pit toilets, and no electricity hold the rustic romance it once did?

I had postponed and re-postponed expeditions all summer for a variety of reasons, not the least of which included the birth of my newest granddaughter, but in September I saw an intriguing photo taken at a likely looking state park in Wisconsin's Driftless Area (basically, motorcyclist heaven). As is my custom, I did practically no research on the park itself, but instead began the hunt for my long-neglected camping gear (more than once finding myself in the garage or basement wondering what it was I was searching for).

I did find my tent, but it's not one of those remarkable modern ones that packs down to the size of a flashlight only to magically bloom into a small cabin, complete with a sitting room, fireplace, and your Beemer's own garage. Instead, mine is an old ripstop nylon and fiberglass mat contraption, with three remaining stakes, tattered zippers, and some poles that had been duct taped together after a sudden blast of wind at an MOA rally in the '90s. It can be crammed into a bag roughly the size and shape of a good-sized Basset hound.

Admittedly, most of the camping gear I was able to resurrect was junk. A pile destined for the dumpster grew steadily: half of a Girl Scouts of America aluminum cooking set, some blobs of what I'm pretty sure were once bars of soap, boxes of damp wooden matches, an empty bottle of Vietnam-era bug juice, and a bunch of miscellaneous left-overs from MREs, like tiny bottles of tabasco sauce, peanut butter (I'm guessing), and rock-hard salt packets.

However, my searches did yield a few much more serviceable items. A barely-used Jet Boil backpacking stove a friend had given me in exchange for boarding his Bonneville one winter was a welcome discovery (complete with a French press!). I also found an inflatable pillow from Exped, which I remembered as being positively luxurious after using a rolled up Aerostich jacket for years. And in the same box was a Thermarest cot, which, although it takes up less space than a loaf of bread, is so diabolically designed, I knew I'd have to practice assembling it in the living room rather than risk trying to figure it out later in a cloud of mosquitos with a flashlight in my mouth.

Totally forgotten and looking almost brand new was a Touratech/Ortlieb collapsible water bowl. About the size and weight of rolled newspaper, it unfolds to hold ten liters of water or anything you'd want to tote to a campsite—really earns its place in any top box. Looking more worse for wear, but still useful, was an army surplus compression stuff sack for my mummy bag. These bags (eBay?) have at least ten straps that can reduce content to half it's normal size.

By the next morning, I was all packed for my impromptu shake-down trip, although with no room for food (I resolved to dine only at five-star convenience stores), and I set off for my camping destination. I hesitate to name the park I headed for, because I don't want to disparage it. It's a cute, well-kept state park featuring a swimming pond and a scenic bluff you can climb using 223 crude, WPA-built steps (I counted them) up to an observation platform that offers scenic vistas stretching out ten miles. Had I done a bit more research and paid more attention to the park map, I would have learned the campsite I chose was located three blocks from an Interstate, four blocks from a state highway, and one block from railroad tracks that carried trains by every two hours (with accompanying air horn at the park road crossing). Not exactly the tranquil setting I normally associate with camping.

Obviously, I passed the night fitfully. I found the cot, although a life-saver compared to sleeping on the ground, had gotten harder to crawl out of than I remembered, being only five inches off the floor. Actually, any maneuvering around in a tent—getting dressed, groping around for glasses, flashlights, and ear plugs, zipping and unzipping jammed zippers to answer nature's calls, chasing mosquitos—had somehow gotten much harder than when I was twenty years younger. Fortunately, my chorus of grunts and expletives didn't bother anyone in the nearly empty campground.

As I heard yet another train approaching, I mentally recounted the string of motels I had passed in nearby Tomah (motto: "Where the Interstate Divides") before

I reached the campground. However, the thought of mounting up and waking some innkeeper to get a room then returning the next day to strike my camp reminded me of a kid chickening out after trying to sleep in the backyard. Instead, my thoughts turned as they seem to do about a hundred times a day to the question, "What am I doing here?"

Maybe this puny camping trip was a belated homage to my father's annual compulsion to pack our family of six into our '58 Mercury station wagon and head up north (his and Mom's queen-size mattress roped to the top). The weeks of mildewed canvas tent, leaking air mattresses, and trips into town for fudge and moccasins (the soles inevitably plastered with burned marshmallows) always teetered on the edge of disaster, but nothing makes family-favorite memories like adversity.

The next day I headed to another state park nearby, Wildcat, which is a wonderful, bluff-top camping and recreation area that sits astride State Highway 33, affectionately known by local riders as "The Tail of the Cow" (Wisconsin's own answer to The Tail of the Dragon). Much quieter, with spectacular views of the lush Driftless coulees, bluffs, and trout streams, this park is clearly one of the gems of Wisconsin's sixty-six-park system.

I broke up the trip home with a stopover to ogle my buddy Zino's new-to-him hydroplane and pet his immaculate V-Rod a little; however, I spent a good deal of my time on the road doing calculations. There was quite a glaring disparity between the hours riding and the hours prepping, setting up, and taking down a campsite, and finally putting everything away where I might be able to actually find it someday. Was it worth it?

Ultimately, I decided moto camping, no matter how much I invest in creature comforts, is always going to be a challenge, maybe more so as I grow even older. But then, so is motorcycling in general, and isn't that part of what makes it our passion? Next summer: Lake Superior and the Porcupine Mountains!

Rideable?

24

THE COLD WAR

As I sit down to write on this middle of November afternoon, we're getting our first snow of the fall. This isn't a snowfall of those fluffy flakes that dance and swirl around beret-capped, deliriously happy townsfolk in a Hallmark Christmas movie, but heavy, wet globs that mean business, dropping straight down, as if pulling a final curtain on autumn. In Wisconsin parlance, this is snow that will "stick."

The snow rings a note of finality to the motorcycle season here, and in an unusual bout of foresight, I actually got my bike Sta-bil-ed, un-batteried, covered, and center stand-ed just in time. However, as usual, I did try to gamely eke out a few last rides as temperatures dropped into the forties. On my last ride (to the storage unit, since my garage has been taken over by my grandson's "Cozy Coup," Big Wheel, and Burley Bee Bike Trailer), it occurred to me how different that ride was from the late fall or early spring rides of my first years of motorcycling.

The Sorel pack boots I wore in my teens were gone, no more newspapers jammed down my pant legs, no more winter parka or wood chopper mitts. No more duct tape around the edges of a bubble face shield, no more wool scarf wrapped around my neck and inevitably trailing behind me like a pitiful pennant proclaiming my rebellion to the oncoming winter (or lack of intelligence, as my dad would suggest). Those days of flirting with frost bite and one scary episode with what I'm pretty sure was hypothermia are thankfully behind me.

Over the ensuing years, cold weather gear has dramatically improved, and although I wouldn't have believed it was possible when I was 21, I actually got smarter and steadily accumulated a pile of stuff that works when it comes to frigid riding. First, I discovered polypropylene long underwear. I can't explain the science of how they insulate, yet breathe, but they're a godsend. Wool socks over polypropylene or silk liners under Thinsulate® boots keep the feeling in my toes, in this case 2000 grams.

Pant liners from Olympia Motosports trap my heat nicely, and over those, my trusty, waxed cotton Cousin Jeremy pants with a bib converter seal the deal. On top, for me the key is layers: long underwear, flannel-lined shirt, heavy fleece or maybe a golf windbreaker to seal in the heat, although I'm on a constant prowl in resale shops for insulated liners. I once found a down-insulated jacket liner but, alas, two sizes too big. I've now settled on an eight-dollar liner apparently once owned by a home builder, although people have started calling me "Bob," since his name is inscribed over the chest pocket.

Keeping one's digits warm and flexible is always a challenge when the temperature heads toward freezing. When I remember to charge them, I wear some Fly Ignitor gauntlet gloves with lithium-ion cells in the cuffs to keep the tops of my hands toasty while grip heaters help underneath. I'm not above using electrics and liked the convenience of one of Aerostich's WarmBibs I tried last year (November *Owners News*, 2021), though, like many electric jacket liners, you're tethered to the bike. In the future, I'm going to investigate battery-powered heat vests. My daughter-in-law, a nurse anesthetist, swears by the one she and her colleagues wear in chilly operating rooms.

I've learned wind chill is really the enemy when it comes to staying comfortable, so I am an unabashed fan of good-sized windshields, especially adjustable, after-market models like those from Madstad. Good quality handguards do more than just protect your hands from brush, and those from MachineArt Moto actually have inserts that can be popped out in warmer weather.

Up top, I pick from a batch of balaclavas for under my helmet. The trick is to find one that breathes, holds the heat, but doesn't make your helmet too tight. Using a full-face helmet with a chin skirt and neck roll surely beats the sixteen-dollar open-face I wore as a kid. A double layer neck gaiter is also nice to have.

That's my strategy for gear when I can't resist pushing the envelope in the spring or extending my riding season in the fall. Of course, I could just drive, but I guess my dad was right: I'll never learn.

25

BIKE-LESS

Early this past spring, I got an offer I couldn't refuse. I had been riding a nifty Honda NC700X for almost exactly a year and had no complaints, but suddenly a guy from Iowa offered me nearly what I paid for it, and being well known for never being able to resist the temptation to dump one bike for something new and different, I let him have the Honda.

Anyone who's been a faithful *Shiny Side Up* reader (gotta be one or two!) knows I have gone through a lot of bikes, many of them BMWs. Apparently, just like my dad was with cars, I'm never completely happy with what I've got. Anyway, as a result of selling the Honda, I've been bike-less for a few months, and it's got me wondering about my fickle nature.

One thing I've come to realize is I like The Hunt. Craigs List, Facebook groups, eBay, newspaper classifieds, the MOA Marketplace—they're all familiar hunting grounds where I've spent (some would say "squandered") time looking for the next best thing. I haven't yet nabbed a prospect at a garage sale like Bill Wiegand, although I have often enquired about dusty two-wheelers resting under old bed sheets or stowed away in a corner in a mess of rusty bicycles, lawn mowers, and snowblowers while I'm browsing for old fishing lures or John Sandford novels.

I do know a guy who has a 2004 Bonneville that he rode one summer then parked in a shed when he started having balance issues. It was one of the 500 turned out with an orange and white gas tank before the plant fire, and I try to drop very subtle queries about its future, but like me, I think he enjoys simply just looking at a bike as much as I do. He had outfitted it with black, leather-fringed saddle bags, a windscreen, and a short sissy bar, which, though not a deal-breaker, diminishes my attraction, and the bike has, God forbid, carburetors. However, that low seat height and distinctive Triumph engine pulse would suit me just fine. Patience.

I also know a guy who I suspect hangs onto a Slash 5 (in a barn no less!) just to torture people like me. To confound me even further, the airhead is dappled with pigeon poop, flecks of straw, and silage dust—sacrilege! It leans dangerously close to an ancient hay rake, which he still tows around behind his Allis-Chalmers. The situation reminds me of a magician who grins while he pretends to cut someone in half.

Even though it pains me to pry open my checkbook when I find a bike I want, I can't say I dislike the actual purchasing. I know the days of dickering and drama over price are over, but during many of my transactions, I've learned a lot of good stuff about motorcycles from genuinely knowledgeable salespersons and owners. And as long as I'm talking about education, I should confess the one time, many years ago, I committed the sin of buying a motorcycle without a test ride. The bike was brought up on a flatbed from Tennessee by a guy named (I swear) "Bubba." I had totally lost my perspective on the eBay buy, thinking what a deal I was making on the Honda

400/4, only to have my mechanic, a mangled carburetor in hand, later point out all the internal insults and injuries the previous owner had visited on what had once been a lovely machine. When I advertised it months later, I put "**AS IS**" in boldface caps, and after the sale, I considered changing my phone number.

The hunt and the purchase are both adventures I enjoy, but once the new-to-me bike is in my garage, I also look forward to the making-it-my-own phase. Every bike I've owned has had its share of idiosyncrasies—a troublesome sidestand (too short/too long/a too-tiny foot), the useless wind screen, the afterthought tail light, the bed of nails or ski-slope saddle—but solving the puzzle of correcting them with my meager shop skills has often been singularly satisfying.

Not far from here, a fellow motorcyclist has devoted his evenings and weekends to painting a mural on the side of his garage. In six-foot letters and radiant colors, it proclaims simply "THE RIDE." Obviously, the main attraction to staying in the saddle is THE RIDE. But is that what it's all about? No, not all. If there's been any benefit to being bike-less for a while, it's that it has reminded me of some of the many, unique pleasures of being a rider: the people you meet, the stories you hear, the places you go (not to mention, the special way you get to see them), and the lessons you learn (about machines and yourself). All of these keep me coming back for more.

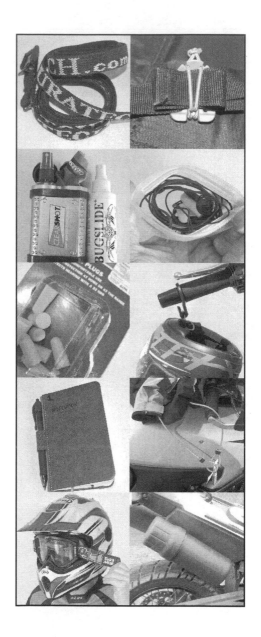

26

LIFE ON LESS THAN $20 A DAY

"That sweatshirt you're wearing is twenty years old!" Actually, my wife was wrong, I've been wearing that sweatshirt for at least thirty years. It's no secret to anyone that knows me that I'm cheap (although I prefer the term *frugal*). Of course, that quality, for some reason, doesn't seem to come into play when it comes to buying motorcycles, where I'm well known for spending too much and selling for too little. However, when it comes to acquiring all those little doodads, thingamabobs, gizmos, and doohickeys that life as a rider seems to require, I spare no expense on, well, sparing expense. So, as I paw my way through my tank bag on a snowy afternoon, here is my list of some favorite moto-peripherals, each for less than twenty dollars.

Touratech Arno Straps, $6.95 each
Rok straps are great for tying down stuff like stuff sacks to your rear rack, but I'd be heartbroken if I lost my Arno straps.

They're not elastic but have a nifty buckle that will not let go, and they take up practically no room in your tank bag (3/4"x 40"). I use them for all kinds of things, on and off the bike. Touratech-USA.com

Helmet Hook, $15.95
If one of these works on your bike, you'll never regret this purchase. Perfectly handy for holding a grocery bag or a helmet while you gear up, it's a simple install. There's even a stainless-steel version now for three dollars more. TheHelmetHook.com

Jacket Caddy, $11.99
Also from the makers of the Helmet Hook is this five-foot, vinyl-coated, steel security cable. It has loops at both ends, won't scratch your bike, and I've found it's great for running through the sleeves of your jacket or chin bar of your helmet and locking them to your bike. Including a padlock will cost you another buck. TheHelmetHook.com

Quick Strap Goggle Mount System, $19.99
Just under my self-imposed red line, this off-road gear drew Mark Barnes's endorsement: "I cannot understand why anyone would want to stick with the OEM strap on their goggles when they can use this setup to make them easy to pull off with one hand, and then replace just as easily (and with precision), while never having to find a place to hang them in the meantime." Revzilla.com

The Tool Tube, $16
On most of the ADV bikes I've owned, a Tool Tube has been a nifty add-on. About a foot long and four inches wide, the Tool Tube fits nicely inside a pannier rack, or on my G 310 GS, it worked well mounted under the rear rack and was a good place to store tire stuff like a mini-compressor or a fuel or water bottle. TheToolTube.com

Bug Slide Travel Kit, $11, and/or Clear Shot All-In-One Lens Cleaning Kit, $13.97

I have both of these. One makes it easier to clean off bug guts from windshields and face shields and leaves a coating that makes it easier to skim them off in the future. The Clear Shot kit keeps the cleaner and cleaning cloths together in a tough looking case, good for a chronic mis-placer like me, and offers some anti-fogging. BugSlide.com, TwistedThrottle.com.

Aisbuger Pocket Notebook, $11.99 (2 pack)

Since I'm a writer, I always carry a little notebook like this (there are hundreds of similar styles and brands), but while most pages are bound, this one has pages at the back that can be torn out for when you want to pass a note in study hall. It can be pretty entertaining to go through one from years ago and read what you were thinking about then! Amazon.com

Molle Dominator Strap Clips, $10.95 (10 pack)

Do you like straps from your tie-downs, backpack, or panniers flapping around as you fly down the highway? Of course you don't, and a ten-pack of these clever, military-approved strap keepers will make you and your bike flapper free. Amazon.com.

3M Disposable Ear Plugs, $2.08

I know, I know, custom-molded ear plugs/ear buds are probably marvelous and much less uncomfortable on a long ride, but they're a lot more than twenty dollars, and I lose everything. I look for 32db on the packages wherever I can find them, and of course, use them for cutting wood, lawn care, leaf blowing, and reading while my wife watches yet another episode of *Flip or Flop*. Walmart.com

Aerostich Earplug Protector, $4

Anyone who's stuck their ear plugs in their pocket knows that, no matter how long they're in there, they're not something you want to stick back in your ears. Aerostich's solution is a clear plastic box, large enough for earplugs and earbuds, that opens with one hand like an old-fashioned coin purse and self-seals to store. Cool, big enough to not misplace, and yes, dirt cheap. Aerostich.com.

This list could be longer, but I've purposely avoided maintenance and repair stuff I carry. Also, the longer this list gets, the more my hard-earned reputation as a cheapskate begins to suffer!

April Fooling

In 2019, BMW Owners News Editor Bill Wiegand asked if I could come up with some sort of spoof for the April issue. He had done one the previous year reporting BMW had merged with Harley-Davidson, and though it was quite humorous, some disgruntled readers misinterpreted the story as being true, so he was a bit reluctant to try another. What follows are my 2018 story and then another from 2019.

27

Product Tested:
Moto-Blazer
by "Chain" Rollofson

Once the snow and ice are gone in Wisconsin, the riding season can usually start around April 1st. However, temperatures that hover in the 30s and dip as low as the teens are always a possibility. What's a rider to do? Sure, there are electric vests, thermal underwear, and fleece, but what's cozier or more environmentally sound than a good old wood fire?

According to inventor Sam "Jackpine" Hoser (pronounced "hoe-'sair"), that was the thinking that led to his new "Moto-Blazer," a rear rack mountable wood burner. "Well, actually," said Hoser, "usin' the Moto-Blazer to heat your backside was kind of a—whadyacallit—bonus. Me and the club guys were just gettin' tired of gettin' rousted by the Crappie Cops (Game Wardens) for startin' campfires wherever we held our field parties, so me and my buddie Ernie came up with a idea of weldin' an old wood stove to his GS so's we could take our campfire wherever we wind up. It was a big hit and warms you up real good when you're ridin', so now we're sellin' 'em."

The Moto-Blazer presents a green solution for cold riding comfort in that it requires no electricity or fuel other than a few pieces of split oak, a renewable energy source. "Once you got good coals, just about anything that'll burn can run it," said Hoser, "even magazines and books. That one by that Riepe guy gave off a lot of hot air."

There were plans to offer the Moto-Blazer online, but after confusion surrounding the product's website, Gotwood?. com," Sam said the heaters will only be sold for now off his back porch. (Bring a bone for Cujo, his Doberman.) The newly-formed company's R&D department is also working on a portable kegerator, again with no reliance on electricity. "The weight problem is a puzzler," Sam quipped. "Them blocks of lake ice get pretty heavy, but you know, we're all about our, um, carb'n footprint. Only problem is, so far Ernie can't get his front wheel to stay down!"

28

Product Review:
DECI-BULL Sound Generator

by April Ersten

Whether you're a fan or not, electronic motorcycles are here to stay and will probably snatch a bigger and bigger role in the market in the future. Even BMW, legendary bastion of the nearly one hundred year old boxer engine, is hinting about an all-electric motorcycle in the next five years. Faster charging rates, longer ranges, and lower prices are sure to be future developments, but so far, all electrics share one problem: they're way too quiet. Sure, there's the sizzle of the chain, some tire hiss, and maybe a gentle hum, but my endorphins, accustomed to taking their cues from a Harley's straight pipes, an Akrapovic hung on a Ducati, or a pair of pea shooter silencers on a Triumph, well, they just roll over and take a nap when I'm on an electric moto. But have no fear, DECI-BULL is here!

Introduced recently by RadNoise, DECI-BULL accessorizes your DC-powered two-wheeler to provide an infinite number of simulated sounds broadcast at an astonishing 250 decibels. Besides providing more safety by making your bike loud enough to startle even the most oblivious, ear-budded pedestrian, the unit offers an unlimited range of sound choices to make everyone, ummm, look at you.

Take, for instance, the "Transportation" menu. From the TFT screen you can scroll through "Semi Tractor Trailer," "M1 Abrams Tank," "1891 Steam Engine (w/whistle)," "German Policia Siren," and many more. Feeling a bit more adventurous? How about the roar of an Lockheed Martin F-35 Lightning II Joint Strike Fighter (w/sonic boom), a Saturn 5 rocket (first stage), or the *Millennium Falcon*?

And that's just one group of ten. Under "Animals," choose "Charging Rogue Elephant," "Screaming Eagle," "Yeti Shriek," or "Timber Wolf Howl." Other groups include selections like "Fingernails on Blackboard," "Grinding Teeth," "That Theme From Jaws," and "Psycho Shower Scene."

Pre-recorded messages are also included in the DECI-BULL options, ranging from a "G" rating for general audiences to "X" (Yeah, pretty sure you could get arrested for some of those.) Owners can also record their own sound effects and messages to play with just a tap of a button, such as "Hey, loser, how about trying the right lane!"

RadNoise's DECI-BULL speakers attach practically anywhere, but ideally clamp to crash bars. Their forward-facing horns, however, do tend to offer some wind resistance and seem to collect a few pounds of insects with each trip. The unit does require three extra heavy-duty twelve-volt car batteries, but for a few dollars more, RadNoise offers a convenient extended top box or a small trailer.

RadNoise founder, Sylvio Primero de Abril, said, "There's nothing else like this on the accessory market for electric motorcycles. We took this to Shark Tank, but unbelievably, they weren't interested—no imagination—so we gave them a big dose of our 'Fraternity Party Toilet Track' on the way out!" The producer of Shark Tank did not offer a response.

The complete DECI-BULL Sound Generator has a MSRP of $3,999, but a contest for the most offensive sound or insult is now running on the RadNoise website, with a first prize of one-half off shipping. For more information, visit radnoise. com.

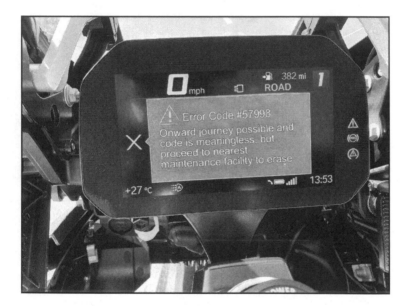

29

BMW Motorrad Reveals Plans For New Electric Models

by April Ersten

Since publicly revealing that BMW Motorrad has a goal of going totally electric by 2030, E-Division Head Designer Heinrich Hochstapler was questioned on what exactly this transition would look like.

"Since BMW sold more carbon-fueled motorcycles in 2021 than ever, enjoying a fifteen percent increase in sales, it will not be an easy undertaking," Hochstapler said. "There is a lot of loyalty to gas-powered bikes, particularly our most popular GS and GS Adventure models; however, we in the design department have already made great progress in creating prototype models that should make the switchover less noticeable."

"For instance," Hochstapler continued, "we don't want to lose the distinctive opposed cylinder profile of our R bikes that has been a hallmark of BMW motorcycles for one hundred years. The new electrics will still have the protruding cylinder heads, though of course, they'll be made of grey plastic, and they'll actually be repurposed as storage compartments for gloves, ear plugs, granola bars, and little spritzer bottles of gasoline to restore that fragrance so many riders covet."

Asked if there will be any other changes in appearance, Hochstapler replied, "The exhaust can, again made of plastic since it will not be functional, will be a great place to store bottle goods, which we know will be especially important to riders like columnist Jack Riepe. There, of course, will also be no need for a gas tank, but buyers of electric GSs can opt to still have the gigantic Adventure tank emulated in a plastic replica that can be used as a computer workstation, fold out garage, or home entertainment center."

Since e-cycles may be lighter than some of the conventional BMW models, special lead weight option packages will be offered to create the same pleasures owners enjoy when moving their motorcycles around in their garages. "They'll be just as fun to pick up after dropping, too," Hochstapler added.

What about all the BMW motorcyclists who have spent so many hours learning to service their own bikes? "We realize there is a certain affinity many motorcycle owners have developed for maintaining their bikes themselves, but electric motorcycles will be mostly maintenance free," Hochstapler explained. "Because of that, we are planning to incorporate meaningless error codes for display on TFT screens that can only be cleared by a certified BMW Master Technician or by purchasing a $500 code reader. Those error codes will admittedly have nothing to do with the operation of the motorcycle," Hochstapler said. "One of our designers has also come up with an ingenious add-on that requires owners to make periodic oil, oil filter, and final drive exchanges every 3,000 miles, although that has no effect on the motorcycle's performance or innerworkings."

Hochstapler admitted there are some special challenges to designers involved in the transition. "The driveshaft on some BMWs, in particular, presents a few problems. The new electrics may use a belt for their final drives, but we're reluctant to delete the look of the iconic driveshaft. Our engineers have been tinkering with developing a faux driveshaft that can be detached and used as a two-foot multipurpose tool. For instance, just like a big Leatherman, the current mock-up transforms into a hatchet, French roast coffee maker, collapsible chair, sleeping cot, bong (where legal), and a small, gas-powered generator for recharging motorcycle batteries when off road or powering an optional wine chiller.

What about re-creating the legendary BMW "growl"? Hochstapler said, "We have already ordered a gross of RadNoise's DECI-BULL sound generators that will presumably take care of that issue. The DECI-BULL sound generator add-on was comprehensively reviewed in a *BMW Owners News* article in last year's April issue, and like everyone, we're very excited about its versatility and, well, its volume."

"Our biggest challenge is to make the new e-motorcycles as close in appearance to the renowned carbon-fueled bikes as possible. They'll look as genuine as me," declared Hochstapler.

At the end of the interview, Hochstapler intimated he had also been working with the BMW Motorrad marketing department on plans for promotions for the new e-motorcycles, particularly the GS models. Another film series similar to *Long Way Round* is reportedly in development, but this one, with a working title of *Long Way Here and There*, would feature GS riders meandering across the US, stopping at every Starbucks and Subway sandwich franchise they come across." Instead of casting Ewan McGregor and Charley Boorman, a majority of male GS riders in an informal survey voted for Scarlet Johansson and Kristen Stewart, but I think they're in talks with former quarterbacks Ben Rothlessberger and Tom Brady, since they won't have anything to do anyway. I guess they both have expressed enthusiasm for the idea of free coffee and being able to stop frequently for bathroom breaks and naps," Hochstapler added.

People

As a moto-journalist, I have often been asked to write profiles about "motorcycle people." Whether their lives have a particular resonance with riders in general or they have been especially innovative in developing products that make our rides safer or more enjoyable, telling these motorcyclists' stories has been a privilege I always look forward to. Here are four that, taken together, represent the kind of resourcefulness, dedication, and adventuresome spirit that will feel familiar to anyone who rides.

30
GLENN STASKY,
INNOVATION MAN

2010. Returning from a business trip in Memphis and headed for home in Sacramento, Glenn Stasky is pushing the speed limit on a desolate section of Highway 50 in Colorado. The sun has just set. An approaching car a mile away begins repeatedly flicking its brights. Annoyed and skeptical his motorcycle's lights could be that bothersome, Glenn nonetheless relents and douses his high beam and auxiliaries. Once the car has passed, he toggles his brights, but by the time the bike's HIDs reach full strength, it's too late. He strikes a dead deer in the road and goes airborne. The car's driver had been trying to warn him.

The cycle comes down, bucking and bouncing, but miraculously stays upright, and Glenn is able to wrench his bike back under control. Shaken, he pulls over to the side of the road, looks up at the stars shining brightly in the thin mountain air, and gives thanks to a higher power.

As Glenn cautiously resumed his two-day journey home to Sacramento, his mind began buzzing in its characteristic problem-solving mode: How could that near fatal accident have been avoided? What would a better lighting system for motorcycles, one that could actually save rider lives, look like?

A self-professed "science geek," Glenn says he's always been fascinated by what makes things work—and how they could be made to work better. "If left alone, I would take everything apart. School taught me the regimen to stay on track to reach a solution and also how to put most things back together again. I remember taking my parent's stereo apart to see what was inside . . . audio became my passion." After making the most of a college scholarship in engineering and then two business degrees, he landed a position with Nakamichi Corporation, then founded his own company in 1990, Clearwater Audio, manufacturing tweeters, woofers, and other amplifier parts. His company grew in size to support thirty employees and built a reputation for American-made quality and service.

As Glenn's career in electronics progressed, so did his enthusiasm for motorcycling. He says he got hooked on bikes after a ride on the back of a BMW R60 when he was just four years old. "A friend of my dad's was a movie stuntman, and he offered me a ride. I never forgot that day, neither did my mom!" His first bike was a Rupp Roadster he received one Christmas, but he soon moved up to Suzuki dirt bikes. Glenn said, "I had seen Evel Knieval a few times, and I became hooked on jumping. Evel even jumped a bunch of cars during an event at Madison Square Garden back in the seventies. Right after seeing him there, I tried even bigger jumps. Three months later, I had a major crash when I was fourteen. Another bike came over a jump, and we hit head-on. My leg was crushed in the middle. I spent two years on crutches while learning to walk again. That was the most humbling time of my life.

It really taught me many lessons. But there has always been a bike in my garage." He has a stable of bikes now, including a new GSA and an Africa Twin.

That love for motorcycling and his career in audio came together in that ill-fated trip coming home from Memphis. Glenn had shipped his bike, along with a truck full of speakers, to his company's biggest client, with the idea of taking a long tour home after delivering the order. Unfortunately, his client broke the news that he had found a new supplier in China. A dark cloud hovered over Glenn's head as he headed for home, where he knew he would have to lay off most of his employees.

Once back in Sacramento, Glenn began research and development on an innovative system for auxiliary motorcycle lighting that featured instant-on LEDs controlled by a dimmer that worked like a volume control for audio. Probing this challenge led to the founding of a new company, Clearwater Lights. Almost ten years later, Clearwater is an international industry leader, now offering seven different levels of light kits for every major brand of motorcycle.

And the incident on the highway in Colorado was not the last time where adversity led Glenn Stasky to innovation. In addition to being a motorcyclist, Stasky also likes car racing. At one practice session at a local track, he witnessed a crash that sadly took the lives of two of his friends. A faulty track warning system failed to alert drivers to trouble ahead, thus preventing first responders from getting to the burning cars. Within a year, he presented a prototype red flag LED system at Daytona which has since been adopted as the new standard and has been installed at tracks all over the US.

Despite Glenn's varied interests and the demanding success of Clearwater Lights, he remains a devoted rider. "Like most riders, I like the feeling of freedom and the connection you get on the open road. Spring rides through the country are some of my favorites. The joy of the different smells that you encounter cannot be experienced in a car. Cagers don't know what they are missing. The only downside of riding would have to be the inattentive drivers and, most of all, the texters."

Glenn's preference in bikes also remains with BMW Motorrad. "The solid and planted feel of a BMW is what impresses me the most. A well-ridden BMW GS can surprise many a sportbike rider. The level of engineering is evident from the drivetrain all the way down to the high beam switch gear."

Glenn also credits the BMW MOA with fueling his affection for BMWs. "I found a copy of the MOA magazine on my dentist's waiting room table many years ago, and my interest in a BMW was ignited. I found that BMW owners are quite different. (Insert cruel joke here . . .) I find it funny when I meet a person for the first time and they hear I ride a motorcycle. They usually say, 'Oh, do you have a Harley?' Some people don't even know BMW makes bikes!"

"BMW owners tend to be very good riders . . . They tend to ride with proper gear, they ride long distances and actually go places. Imagine that. When I ride, it is usually only with one or two other riders. Quite often I ride alone. I like the friendly feel of the MOA group, and I really look forward to seeing our friends from around the country when we attend the MOA rally. We have some great memories from these events. I will always be a member."

As for the future, Glenn Stasky continues to ride and explore innovations that will make motorcycling safer and more enjoyable for all riders. He recently completed an 8,100 mile trip over some of the hottest areas of the country to test a prototype for a miniature air conditioning system for motorcycles and race cars. The system features a biometric control system that monitors an operator's vital signs, varying compressor and pump speed as needed. He said, "There is something to be said about fifty-five degree water pumping around your chest when it is 105 degrees outside."

Snatching innovation from the jaws of vexation is a distinguishing quality of Glenn Stasky's life, but isn't it the challenge for all motorcyclists? How many other lifestyles put its adherents into such a potentially risky, physically and mentally demanding, yet singularly satisfying pursuit? I'm sure the community of riders, in general, and MOA members, specifically, are proud to welcome Glenn Stasky as one of their own.

31
ARIANNE MIHALKA:
LIKE FATHER, LIKE DAUGHTER

People develop a passion for motorcycles for many reasons—the freedom, the exhilaration of speed, the focus demanded of mind and body to pilot a bike safely—but for a rider like Arianne Mihalka, riding her RT keeps her in touch with her father's spirit.

"Being my father's daughter, I grew up around motorcycles all my life. My dad always had a motorcycle, and I loved riding with him since I was very young. Back in Venezuela and after he moved to Miami and then to Sykesville in Maryland, I always rode with him when I had a chance, but I was always on the back of his bike. Then in 2013 I had some big changes in my life. First, I was going through a divorce, and I decided it was time to get my own bike and do something fun for myself.

My dad came to Florida, and we went to BMW Motorcycles of Fort Lauderdale, where my dad had worked for many years, and he helped me choose my first bike. My dad was very supportive and excited about me getting a bike, and then the worst happened, a few weeks later my dad passed away; it was very unexpected. Since then, besides loving to ride, being on a bike is the best way to be close to him." Arianne added, "It's in my DNA."

It was no wonder Arianne's attraction to motorcycling had begun with her father. Paul Mihalka was a two-time Venezuelan and one-time All-South-American motorcycle racing champion in what was the largest engine class of the time. Additionally, Paul was an inspiration and mentor to Jim Ford, author of *The Art of Riding Smooth*.

"I always admired my dad for his passion for motorcycles, and I loved riding with him, but I only understood why he liked it so much this last year, when I finally made it out of Florida and did a nine-day trip with my boyfriend, Brian Gillespie, who also rides a BMW." Arianne and Brian rode the Blue Ridge Parkway and through the Shenandoah National Park, and she said she "loved every minute of it."

Arianne's connection with her father's history also extends to the brand of bikes she's had. "I grew up around BMWs all my life. My dad did 1.2 million miles on BMWs, and being an engineer myself, I really appreciate their design and performance. Only a rider since 2013, Arianne's first BMW was a 2012 F 800 R. "It was a great starting bike, but three years later it was time to upgrade. My next bike was a 2009 R 1200 R, I ride a lot with the Gold Coast Beemers, our local BMW club, and finally it was easy to keep up with the group. I really enjoyed that bike, but last year we were doing longer rides, and I started thinking about how nice it would be to have some wind protection and more storage, so I got a 2011 R 1200 RT. I just LOVE this bike. This one is a keeper for a long time."

One of Arianne's earliest memorable rides was as a passenger on her dad's bike when they ran Skyline Drive in

West Virginia. Another highpoint was riding with Jim Ford on his "invisible roads" the day of a memorial ride that Jim organized in the Appalachian Mountains for her father.

"Since I started riding, most of my rides have been local in Florida. We have our annual club ride to Mount Dora . . . some beautiful roads and a great group of people. Arianne also mentioned the BMW winter rally in Starke, Florida, and going through the Ocala National Forest. "On my last trip to the BMW MOA National Rally in Lebanon, Tennessee, we took the Auto Train from Sanford, Florida, loaded the bikes, and got off the next day in Virginia. The train was a wonderful experience, and we then headed to the rally, going through Skyline Drive, the Blue Ridge, little Switzerland, and the Tail of the Dragon."

Following her father's advice, Arianne says she is a firm believer in ATGATT. She said she's only had one close call so far, a run-off caused by some loose gravel on a curve. "Luckily, the side of the road was sand and grass, and besides a good scare, I didn't go down." Arianne says there are many things she loves about riding, including what she called "the best therapy," the feeling of freedom, the adventure, and sharing those adventures with her boyfriend Brian and a great group of friends. She added that she dislikes traffic, distracted drivers, and the heat and humidity of Florida in the summer.

As for the future, Arianne says she has a full bucket list. "I love riding and going on trips. We organize a one day ride a month with the club; those are a fun way to catch up with friends, and we try to go to different destinations every time, but I definitely hope to be able to do longer trips in the US—so many beautiful places, national parks to see. I also would love to ride overseas in Europe, visiting places where my family is from, Hungary, Poland, Austria, and Switzerland." Truly Paul Mihalka's daughter, she would also like to try racing someday. As her father always told her, "You don't stop riding because you get old —you get old because you stop riding."

32

A MOMENT WITH
ANDREW SERBINSKI

Whether we realize it at the time or not, everyone probably has had their own "watershed moments"—those serendipitous crossroads of experience that, as Robert Frost once wrote, "made all the difference."

One watershed moment for Andrew Serbinski occurred in 1975. Armed with a fresh industrial design degree from the Pratt Institute, Serbinski was living in Japan, designing the first of the plain paper copiers for Ricoh. He received a dated copy of *Cycle Magazine* forwarded by his parents, and on the cover was what has now come to be considered an iconic motorcycle, the BMW R 90 S.

Serbinski writes, "I was stunned. In one fell swoop BMW produced something radical—silver smoke paint, a bikini fairing, elegant removable side cases, dual disc front brakes, racer-like tail, and a CLOCK in the cockpit. It just looked right—beautifully proportioned, with strong, simple, glossy shapes perched atop rounded, dull cast aluminum cases. What a forward-looking and beautiful piece it was from such a conservative company... thoughts of it kept me awake at night."

After returning to New York later that year, Serbinski took his life savings of $3,800 and purchased his own Daytona Orange R 90 S. "I had to have one. For years it was my magic carpet ride out of the city—a constant source of pleasure and pride." He still has that bike and says, "After thirty-four years, it still makes me stare."

Following years of working as a design consultant for American and Japanese interests, in the '80s Andrew Serbinski founded Machineart Industrial Design (MaMo) based in Frenchtown, New Jersey. The company produced designs for an eclectic collection of products—medical devices, sports equipment, powersports accessories, packaging, graphics, and housewares—all aimed at generating what Serbinski describes as an "emotional response on top of being rationally designed for a purpose . . . creating desire for the stuff people want and need to live, work, and play." One of Machineart Industrial Design products, a cervical immobilization device for use by EMTs, was showcased in a Museum of Modern Art exhibit.

But motorcycles have never been far from Serbinski's mind. In 1996 his company designed a concept bike called the Machineart-Kawasaki MK9. The design study was based on a Ninja chassis and, in Serbinski's words, was "intended to demonstrate how a ubiquitous Japanese four-cylinder layout could be designed to be desirable at first glance."

Serbinski claims, "Motorcycles that have lots of personality, like Ducatis, were the vision of one or a few people rather than a committee—which is how the Japanese ones are designed. When the Japanese do a new product, they gather competitive product pictures together and put them in a kind of matrix of styles to evaluate. The problem is they're using existing products to capture visual information, and if they're designing something new, they shouldn't base it solely on what exists now, because it's already old stuff."

The MK9 emphasized the idea of visual "flow" and earned a 1997 Industrial Designers Society of America Gold award, not to mention international attention and more calls for innovative motorcycle studies. Serbinski and his staff developed styling concepts for Ducati's ST4 and a new "Super Monster" power cruiser, and the Machineart portfolio continued to expand with design concepts for three variations of a gas/electric hybrid motorcycle for the start-up eCycle (ecycle.com).

In 2005, Andrew and friend and Master BMW technician Tom Cutter, of the famous Rubber Chicken Racing Garage, went to sample the new 2005 BMW R 1200 GS. Serbinski said, "The new GS was a big improvement over the previous model, with lighter weight, increased power, and very light handling. But, I had to say to Tom afterwards, 'This is a creature only Godzilla's mother could love!'" Serbinski and Machineart viewed the new bike as an opportunity to develop a new design for the GS that could be simply "beautiful." Serbinski bought an R 1200 GS and got to work translating the bike into the "Machineart dialect."

Finding the looks of the GS "hunky, rough and tumble, and broadly capable," Serbinski recognized that the majority of GSs are used as sport tourers and sportbikes on-road, which makes their dirt bike looks inconsistent with their use. After hearing standard GS owners saying they appreciated the GS's versatility, comfortable upright riding position, luggage hauling capacity, and comfort options but weren't enamored with "the two-wheeled Land Rover look," Machineart designers began thinking about a new GS platform that would look right for sport riding without sacrificing the bike's "off-road goodness." The GSM was born.

"I began sketching GSM ideas with the intent of retaining the GS's muscle tone but making it leaner, more finely chiseled, smaller and lighter looking," Serbinski said. Continuous "flow" was a design goal. "It's a classical notion of guiding a viewer's eyes over a sculpture, an automotive form, or around a painting in a way that enables one to absorb the whole by taking it in uninterrupted." Serbinski admits the "Land Rover aesthetic with its winches, jerry cans, racks, and spare tires stuck all over" has its appeal, but it's not for everyone.

The re-design for the GS began in three dimensions, with foam, plastic, and clay mockups following preliminary sketches, aided by 3D printing of components. Elements of the new look included cylinder guards, fenders, and a different kind of windscreen, and in order to make the study financially viable, these add-ons were prototyped into production pieces that could be marketed. The Machineart GSM thus became a development platform for a host of products now familiar to GS owners, including the Mudsling rear fender, X-Head cylinder guards, Slipstream sport shields, and most recently, ADVance hand guards, all offered by Andrew Serbinski's sister company founded in 2007, MachineartMoto.

Side by side, the GSM looks smaller, lighter, more agile, and faster, according to Serbinski, without changing underlying frame and fuel tank mass or sacrificing the elements of toughness, versatility, and customizability. "Flow" is achieved through the long and narrow red body panels, while understating the flat black fuel tank. "Color is used to draw attention to the sense of movement, and parts that should recede are dark," said the designer.

At rallies where it is displayed, riders ask, "How much does it cost, and is a kit available?" The answer is "It's a design study and not available." Although there might be a worldwide market for a GSM, Serbinski feels the number of units sold would be too low and the costs too high to make production cost-effective. However, the MachineartMoto products for the BMW GS line spawned by the GSM study, along with similar products for Triumph Tigers, KTMs, and the Honda Africa Twin are available from major vendors and from the MachineartMoto website.

Andrew Serbinski and MachineartMoto's achievements and contributions are remarkable, all the more so when considering it all started with the one fortuitous moment evoked by a BMW motorcycle.

33

MARINA ACKERSON:
A RIDER'S RIDER

At noon on Saturday of a rally in Des Moines, I was in a momentary fix. Handcuffed with a steaming hot burrito and glass of Leinenkugels, all the tables in the food area were taken. Spying a woman eating by herself at a table for four, I asked if I could join her. What followed was a long conversation about her, motorcycles, and riding that made me feel I had met the quintessential motorcyclist. A former corporate consultant and instructor on Problem Solving and Decision Making, Project Management, and Interpersonal Communications, her history of rider training and teaching, her self-reliant, nation-spanning touring, and her obvious love of motorcycling would be inspiring to any rider. Meet Marina Ackerson . . .

What was your first motorcycle experience?

My first motorcycle experience was in 1975 on the back of my husband's used Yamaha. We went two-up to Myrtle Beach, wearing blue jeans and jean jackets. By the time we got back home, I thought my teeth were rattling out. I rode on the back of his motorcycles (the rest BMWs) for ten years.

Was that what got you hooked?

I guess I was hooked on where motorcycles could take me, the people I met along the way, and going places I would otherwise never have gone. Plus, the great feeling of wind on my face. I was really hooked when I took the MSF course, put the motorcycle in first gear, my feet on the pegs, and rolling on the throttle. I got a grin on my face from ear to ear, and it's never gone away.

What was the first bike you rode, and what kinds of bikes have you ridden over the years?

My first bike was a 1985 R 80, black. I called her "Black Beauty." I put 100K on that motorcycle, sold it to my daughter in 1995, who put another 100K on it. I have had six motorcycles over the years. My next was a used 1997 Red F 650 Funduro, which I bought to go to Alaska in 1999. Next was a 1995 R 1100 R, silver with a red seat. In 2007, I bought my most favorite bike, a black 2007 R 1200 R. I called her "Spirit." Next, a 2009 F 650 GS twin, red. I put 100K on her, too (see odometer photo the day I sold her). I am now riding a 2016 F 700 GS twin, burnt orange, along with a 2007 Suzuki 650SV.

What do you like most and least about riding?

Riding still puts a smile on my face and takes me to new places where I meet new friends. I still love the wind on my face. It keeps me away from the anti-depressants the doctor wanted to put me on when my husband passed away in 2005. He was my riding partner for twenty years. I told the doctor, "No thanks, I'll just go ride my motorcycle."

What I like least about riding a motorcycle is the maintenance. When you put a lot of miles on, there is always maintenance to do, and I am no mechanic. Thank goodness for dear friends and some of the BMW dealers. A special thanks to SANDIA BMW in Albuquerque, where I bought my 2016. They treat me with the same respect they show the "guys" and always do good work for me. They took me in for service without an appointment when I just pulled in there after the national this year, even though they were very busy with a tour group coming through.

Also, I don't like crossing the plains. The roads are straight and flat, and you wear out yourself and your tires. Miles and miles of nothing but miles and miles, and I've done every route from north to south in the US and Canada. Since I live in Michigan and love riding in the West, I still sometimes do it. I also leave a bike in Albuquerque sometimes and fly out to ride.

Why a BMW?

Being very short, the BMW is light weight, well-balanced, and smooth and has good handling and brakes. It does what I want it to do and takes me where I want to go.

How have your feelings/attitudes toward riding evolved over the years?

Not much, I don't think. I still love to do it and hope my health holds out so I can continue. I'm maybe more picky about who I ride with. Also, being retired, I have the luxury of time, so I can hold up for a day or two if necessary to avoid bad weather.

Where have you ridden?

By 1990 I had ridden in twenty-seven states, Canada, and Mexico, including a Pancho Villa all women's ride to Mazatlan, crossing at El Paso. Since then I have covered forty-nine states, some of the provinces in Canada, and states in Mexico, including a Rawhyde adventure to the Baja from Tecate,

California, ferrying across to the mainland at Topolabamba to Creel and back into Arizona. It was an adventure ride where I was in over my head with a '97 Funduro with dual sport tires instead of knobbies. I spent lots of time in the cab of the the chase vehicle, but it's a trip I will never forget. Hawaii is the only state I haven't ridden a motorcycle in. I have my 100, 200, and 300,000 mile badges from the MOA and am working on 400K. The good news is I still love doing it; the bad news is I am getting old.

What is your most memorable trip?

There are so many, but a few to mention are the ten weeks in Alaska, the adventure ride in the Baja, and trips to Sonora with friends and the Chain Gang. Also I have great memories of riding the Pacific Coast from San Diego to Washington State, Rocky Mountain National Park, and a short ride in Florida, when the sky opened up and we got caught in the rain the rest of the way back to our rental. We both had big grins on our faces when we took our helmets off. Sometimes you don't have to go far to be totally happy with the ride.

Training experience?

I taught motorcycle safety in the Detroit metro region for fifteen years, both novice and experienced rider courses. I took the Reg Pridmore and Rob Beach RATS and Reg Pridmore Class high speed riding course at Grattan raceway in Michigan five years in a row, and of course, the three day Rawhyde adventure school in California. I think more training is better and believe it has saved me from accidents along the way.

Have you had any close calls or other unfortunate events?

Yes. In 2008 I was riding from the 49er Rally to a friend's house on the coast on a twisty, tree-lined mountain road when a deer jumped out from the ditch and into my front wheel. It threw me onto the loose, black dirt shoulder where

I kept it up for a few seconds and then laid it down and spun out on the road. The deer, according to those riding behind me, flew over, kicked my helmet, and broke the flip-up on my helmet, so I was briefly without vision 'til it flipped back down. I thought I was going to walk away clean, but my left foot got pinned under the rear peg, so people had to help me get out from the bike. An ambulance came and took me to the hospital to check me out. No scratches, no broken bones, just some pulled ligaments in my left leg, but it hurt pretty good. Thanks go to Ozzie and Emmy from Ozzie's BMW, who came to pick me up, take me to their house, and let me stay there for a couple days. I then flew to Tucson, where another BMW friend put me up for a few days, and then another friend drove me to Deming, New Mexico, where I had my other motorcycle. I count myself very lucky I wasn't hurt worse. My 1200 was totaled. Don't want to go through that again! A big thanks to my BMW motorcycle "family."

The other was on my 1997 Funduro. I had camped at the Gila Hot Springs in New Mexico. I packed up and left early in the morning and was riding through Emory Pass when I realized I was "freewheeling." The curvy, two lane mountain road didn't have much shoulder, but I got the bike stopped, got off. The chain was just hanging. No cell service of course, so I waited for someone to come by. A couple from California touring the area stopped. They insisted I take everything off the bike put it in the trunk of the car, and they drove me to a spot where I had cell service and called a tow truck. It took a while for him to show up. He said when he found out it was a motorcycle he got a special trailer to pick it up. He was a rider himself, and he looked over the bike and determined I had lost a sprocket. We looked up and down the road to find it, but we never did. We weren't sure what we were going to do, but he called a few motorcycle shops in Silver City. I realized we were close to Deming, New Mexico, where my friend, Don Cameron, lives. He owned the BMW shop there for years. Don said to bring it over. I wrote an article about this, and it was published in the *Owners News*, titled "Some People Will Give You the Sprocket off Their Motorcycle."

Being an expert on problem solving, how has that affected your approach/history with motorcycles?

I like to call it "critical thinking." Preparing for a ride, both the motorcycle and myself. Making sure all the maintenance is taken care of . . . to take a line from the *Blues Brothers*, "Tires are good, brakes are fair, pack of lucky strikes, and cheap sunglasses" and off you go. I guess I would say be prepared. Cell phone, anonymous book, some tools. Know yourself and how many miles you can travel in a day without getting exhausted. Try to assess the situation if something happens, determine potential causes.

What kinds of advice would you give other riders?

Know yourself. Ride within your limits. Take a safety course and any other courses you can.

Have you encountered any special challenges as a female rider?

One challenge is people not taking you seriously. Men tend to want to give advice to a woman they would never give to a man. Sometimes it's the opposite. I have another little story. I rode from my house in Michigan to Albuquerque in two 750-mile days. On the second day, when I was getting near my daughter's house in Albuquerque, I pulled off the expressway at a rest area and called her. When I hung up the phone there was a man standing there, staring at me. I asked if I could help him, and he just looked at me, and he said, "You've been doing this a long time, haven't you? I've been following you for three states." My message for other women who ride would be, "It's just one mile at a time."

What are your future plans in terms of riding?

My bucket list includes Hawaii and New Zealand, both the north and south islands. I plan to keep doing what I've always done. Look for rallies to go to and new places to ride, meeting new people along the way.

GUEST WRITER:
MOLLY MILROY

Why do people like riding on motorcycles? Last year I ran across a short essay written by Molly Milroy that, aside from its simple elegance, I felt came close to answering that question. Although the evocative images she captures from her first ride after a number of years are sharply drawn, it's more the exuberant tone of her writing that urged me to share it with my readers...

34

I FORGOT

BY MOLLY MILROY ("MRS. SUBJECTIVE"*)

Last week was the first time I rode on the back of a motorcycle in more than ten years. It was the first time I rode with my husband, Aerostich's "Mr. Subjective,"* whose life revolves around the activity, or what he would call "a social good." In my years of knowing him, he has talked more about motorcycling and the benefits of motorcycling than anything else. The first time he launched into a monologue about it, I thought he was a bit off, even a little weird. Who was this guy, so passionate about motorcycling? I already knew he was a philosopher. That is one of the main attributes that drew me to him. But I didn't understand his drive (pun intended). I was intrigued.

Throughout the years, I have heard him talk about these beneficial factors to countless people—friends and family, strangers, and more. And he'll talk about it anywhere. At a dinner party. On the airplane. Even at our wedding.

So when we headed up Hwy 61 in Duluth the other day, I knew that I was in good hands. But I was still a little scared. It had been so long since I had been on a bike, and even though I have my motorcycle license and owned my own motorcycle once, I hadn't ridden in ten years. And I forgot.

During our ride, I was surprised how quickly I went from feeling scared to feeling alive, calm, and more in tune with the present moment. It dawned on me that I had forgotten so many things about motorcycling that I liked, the ones that drew me to get my own license eleven years ago.

I forgot what it felt like to see the world from a new perspective, one without windows intercepting my vision.

I forgot what it felt like to notice things on the streets I have driven down countless times. Mouldings on buildings. A lady sitting on her front porch step smoking a cigarette. The child learning how to ride a bicycle.

I forgot what it felt like to feel the wind push against my body.

I forgot what it felt like to fly.

I smelled the fresh spring flowers and the fresh spring rain which had just come down earlier that day. So much freshness is not something you encounter when sealed in your car.

I connected. I smiled at people. The elderly couple at the stop light next to us. I waved. She waved. And gave me a little grin. And the younger couple at the stop light on the way home. They smiled and looked at us a little quizzically. I even stuck my hand down to wave at another biker as we passed in opposite directions.

I also connected with my husband. Feeling my body press against his. His left hand patting my left leg, letting me know he was thinking of me.

I tasted.

I tasted freedom. And the fresh Lake Superior windblown air.

I heard.

I heard the sound of the bike rumbling against the pavement. I heard the birds chirping in the trees. I heard the wind as it brushed against my helmet.

At one point he said, "We're whimsical."

I liked that.

I forgot all of these things. And that short ride up Hwy 61 reminded me and solidified everything he's been telling me about riding since I met him; motorcycling is a human and a social good. It brings us closer to others. It gives us better awareness of our surroundings. It helps one to see more details and to be aware at all times. It makes us better all-around citizens and car drivers. How one can connect with others, and oneself, easier. And how motorcycling can bring one to the present moment, experiencing all of the senses at once, in a new, and transformative way.

All of these attributes make me a better car driver. I am now even more aware of those around me, looking out for others who are not in cars; motorcyclists, bikers, walkers, etc. Motorcycling is a solo activity, one which connects one to others in a profound way.

I don't love motorcycling the way Mr. Subjective does. I probably never will. But I have tasted a new sense of freedom within and I want more of it. It's been five days since we first took that ride together. And three of those days, I've asked him to take me again. I have drunk the Kool-Aid. There's no going back and I'm a better person for it.

"Mr. Subjective" is Andy Goldfine, founder of Aerostich Riderwear.

Reviews

After buying my first set of real motorcycle gloves more than twenty years ago, I decided to try writing a review and submit it for publication. When it appeared in print, I was hooked on seeing my name in a motorcycle magazine byline. Editors like Sandy Hughes, Vince Winkel, Mary Baker, and Bill Wiegand encouraged me to do more reviews, which eventually led me to do features, profiles, and finally, my own column. My policy, as far as reviews, has been to only accept products or books for review that I'm already pretty sure I can endorse, and here are four of my favorite reviews, two for books, two for products, where it was easy to lend my support . . .

35
DIRTY DINING,
AN ADVENTURER'S COOKBOOK

Whenever I have been bivouacked on a motorcycle trek in the past, my approach to cooking can be best be expressed by a turn of the old Nike slogan: Just Don't Do It. My dinner fare has usually featured trail mix, some questionable beef jerky, and possibly a squashed banana, and the most challenging meal preparation has involved trying to open a bottle of craft beer with a screwdriver.

My aversion to cooking could stem from the way I was raised. Although I loved my mom dearly, her primary concern when it came to cooking our food was to immolate any conceivable lifeforms that might be lurking there, hence pork chops could easily be mistaken for portions of a catcher's mitt. My dad's cooking was confined to grilling hamburgers or steaks, where often keeping the martini glass filled took preference over attention to cooking technique.

So it was with some hesitation that I accepted the assignment to review Lisa Thomas's new cookbook, *Dirty Dining, An Adventurer's Cookbook*. What I found, however, was a delightful guide to cooking on the road that I think anyone, even a hopeless kitchen cast-out like me, could not only enjoy reading at home but could also find imminently useful on the trail.

It would be next to impossible to find a greater authority on coping with life on the road than Lisa Thomas. She and her husband, Simon, have moto-trekked through at least seventy-eight countries and six continents over the last fourteen years, both recognized as being the foremost voices in motorcycle adventuring. Their reputation has been established through frequent contributions to adventure magazines, broadcast media, and through their "2RideTheWorld" website, and they are testers and spokespersons for a number of premier gear marquees, including being named as Official BMW Motorrad Brand Ambassadors since 2011.

Although only released this year, *Dirty Dining* has already earned some sterling recommendations, even one from adventure icon Ted Simon (*Jupiter's Travels*). Lisa explains, "This book is not intended to be a gourmet cooking guide or even a country-by-country recipe book...This book gets down to the nitty-gritty of how to make do when there is nothing much around to eat. The recipes in this book are for when you are out in the 'boonies,' where fresh produce is scarce to non-existent, or high up in the Altiplano riding at 15,000 feet. Maybe you're in the desert at 122°F (50°C) or struggling in the sodden tundra fighting elephant-sized mosquitos. Or perhaps you are just too plain broke and tired to engage your imagination and work out what the hell to do with that tin of tuna and other basic items that you have with you!"

The book begins with six brief sections on fundamentals, giving time-tested recommendations on everything from

"The Pantry" (herbs, flavorings, and versatile foodstuffs) to cooking methodology to "Weaponry." It's obvious that all of Lisa's recommendations are the result of her experiences coping with the conditions and space and weight limitations that adventure motorcycling presents.

After valuable lists of tips on health, safety, and environmental concerns, the "meat" of the book begins, featuring twenty-six tantalizing but simple recipes. The recipe portion of the book, however, is more than simply lists of ingredients and instructions. Each chapter featuring a dish begins with an evocative narrative from one of the exotic locations the Thomases have visited, accompanied by a series of gorgeous photos. Lisa shares anecdotes from many of her and Simon's waypoints, from Nepal to New Zealand, giving the armchair tourer a strong sense of place and what it's like to "Ride the World." A sampling of the variety of tempting recipes includes "Orange Pork," "Make-Do Mongolian Stew," "Meat-Fest Asado," and "Sardine Spaghetti."

To see if even a culinary klutz like me could use *Dirty Dining*, I chose Lisa's "Spanish Tortillas" for a road test. Lisa intimates that she and Simon favored this recipe on a trek through the Annapurna Mountain Range. Her photos and description convey the beauty and peacefulness of a sleepy village, savored over a simple meal and a Nepali beer called "Everest." As with most of the dishes in this book, the list of ingredients is short, the required gear is minimal (small frying pan, sauce pan, Dragonfly™ cookstove or campfire), and the preparation time is brief (twenty minutes). Under "Method" Lisa offers clearly stated steps, with all kinds of special tips obviously generated from experience. Lisa's Spanish Tortillas combine potatoes, onions, and eggs, which make something much like an omelet. Although my tortillas didn't look quite as appetizing as those pictured in the book, topped with a little cheddar and a slice of tomato, they hit the spot. (Not being anywhere near Nepal, I substituted a bottle of Two Hearted Ale from Bell's Brewery in the UP.)

Lisa Thomas's *Dirty Dining, An Adventurer's Cookbook* is available from online booksellers, and more information and a sample dish recipe video (a scrumptious salvation for my poor squashed banana) is available at 2RIDETHEWORLD. com.

36

CORNERING CONFIDENCE: THE FORMULA FOR 100% CONTROL IN CURVES

When I was young and stupid, I'm pretty sure I equated experience with competency. For example, to learn how to play the drums, I spent hour after hour alone in my bedroom, banging away to the same, simple rock songs every night. (My parents were saints.) It's only now (I still drum) that I've realized if I'm serious about improving on the drums, I will have to start over on some techniques, with guidance from experts.

When it came to motorcycling, I think I subconsciously reasoned that the more I rode, the better I would be at riding. It's only when I became older, and I hope wiser, did

I realize that, although experience is valuable, competency, confidence, and even enjoyment using a specific skill only come when experience is integrated with knowledge. Even after decades of drumming, I still go back to books, lessons, and YouTube videos, and when it comes to motorcycling, skills books by Hough, Parks, Hahn, Ford, Code, and others continue to crowd my bookcase. The newest and a most welcome addition to that bookcase is *Cornering Confidence* by Jon DelVecchio.

Though DelVecchio came later than some to riding, his passion for developing and refining his skills led him to certification as a MSF coach and then later to the founding of his own "Street Skills" rider courses, which continue to earn accolades. *Cornering Confidence* is not an introduction to all aspects of riding, but as its title suggests, it is rather a sharply focused, advanced guide on how to enhance motorcycling skillsets for the curves. I'm sure I'm not the only one who's amazed to watch expert racers pitch over and drag a knee through a sharp TT corner, but this book is about street riding, and through its twelve chapters of explanations, photos, diagrams, and highlighted "Core Concepts," DelVecchio reveals how any rider can move to the next level of competency, confidence, and enjoyment when attacking corners.

I must admit, until I read this book, I had not given much thought to using body position in curves, which I learned helps maximize traction and provides more of a safety margin for the unexpected. I also had not appreciated how much braking, accelerating, leaning, and steering can affect suspension and thus control (and how I could mitigate those effects!). DelVecchio's overriding principals of "Flat and Straight," "Kissing the Mirror," smooth brake/ throttle transitioning, and trail braking for better control were revelations to me and have changed the way I ride.

For example, following DelVecchio's clear instructions on leaning the bike less while shifting upper body positions more in a corner felt a little awkward at first but made complete sense. Eventually, playing a more active role in maneuvering the bike decreased my anxiety and increased my self-confidence. Integrating DelVecchio's unconventional advice on trail braking is more complicated, particularly with the author's emphasis on using the front brake and continuing to brake after entering a turn, but with the book's explanations and suggested exercises, I hope to eventually reach the goal of what he calls "unconscious competence" with this technique.

As Jon DelVecchio notes in *Cornering Confidence*, if you ride for ten years with no attempt to increase your skills knowledge, you're really just riding the same year ten times. And although there will always be room for more skills improvement, his book is one way to make each ride safer, smoother, and more fun.

Cornering Confidence: The Formula for 100% Control in Curves is available from most online booksellers.

37

An Upgrade for
"The Transformer"

Someone asked me recently what has been my favorite of all the gear I have used and reviewed over the past ten years. It's a tough question, since I've had the opportunity to test quite a few pieces of high-quality gear, including protective clothing, accessories, and miscellaneous farkles, but since they are such an integral part of my ride, I've always looked forward to the chance to try different helmets. I've worn a bunch of them, from high-end models to lesser lids I refused to even write about because of their poor quality, but one that sticks out as a favorite was Nolan's N44 Crossover, first introduced about eight years ago.

Kind of an oddity at the time, the N44 was one of the first helmets to feature a drop-down sun shield, but more notably, also one of the first to offer a new approach to versatility with a design that, through interchangeable parts, could be used in six different configurations. I think at the time Nolan called the N44 a "modular" or a "crossover," but I thought "transformer" was an even better descriptor. I also called it a "helmet for all seasons," since I felt it was a great fit for a Wisconsin rider like me where, when hearing praises or complaints about the weather, natives will often say, "Give it a day . . . "

Until its shelf life expired, on hot days I wore the N44 with just the chin guard, vented peak, and no face shield, lowering the dark UV400 sunscreen when I wasn't in a shady stretch. Four big intakes on the crown and exhaust vents also helped keep my noggin cool. When I was feeling nostalgic, I could use the N44 with no chin guard or face shield, and poof—a '60s-style three-quarter open face. Pushing the riding envelope in November and March, the top air intakes could be closed, while the face shield, chin guard, chin curtain, and neck roll eliminated frostbite, although admittedly, there was little that could be done about snow.

Nolan's newest version of their forward-thinking N44 is the N70-2 GT, and although it looks a lot like the old N44 and has the same quality Nolan fit and finish, there have been some significant updates. I got an N70 dressed in the newly-offered brilliant hi-vis chartreuse, now a ubiquitous color for anyone working around traffic; it is also available in white, black, and two graphics designs. It still has the familiar detachable chin guard, which locks in solidly with stainless latches and is claimed to offer as much protection as that of a full-face. By removing the chin guard, I can slip the helmet on and off without removing my glasses, although of course, one drawback is it's easy to misplace that part (I once drove off with mine on the pillion seat; fortunately, replacements are available).

The drop-down sun shield, one of my favorite features, has a new, larger shape and has three detents for position. It's scratch and fog resistant, so no problem going without the face shield. A word about that face shield: I have not tried any full-face or modular helmet that has a wider field of view. In fact, I can't see the edges of the helmet in peripheral vision. Like the N44, the N70-2 GT's face shield has three detents, one at about an inch open, a second at the top of the face opening, and a third fully retracted. In my review eight years ago, I noted that the system for removing and installing the shield is one of the most user-friendly and quickest I've ever tried, enabling fast change-outs for weather variations and bug issues; that has not changed.

I have never been able to understand why some helmet makers make a pinlock insert an option. Nolan includes one at no extra cost, and although it can be kind of a pain to install, I don't know why anyone wouldn't just leave it on, since it's the best preventative for fogging in any temp.

Another unique characteristic of the N44 and now the N70 (actually of all Nolans) is the "Microlock2" chin strap latch. A notched tab slides into a receiver and locks; lifting a lever releases it. This patented feature is quicker, glove-friendly, and just as secure as the D-rings other manufacturers favor, but doesn't work with on-board helmet locks. However, Nolan thoughtfully includes a helmet strap "TBar" which slips into the Microlock2 and provides an attachment for most helmet locks or cable locks built in on many bikes.

I still have my old Nolan N44 for comparison, and I found the newest version a definite upgrade in comfort. From the padded strap to the removable neck roll to the plush liner, the newest crossover felt snug and comfy, although I found I do have to sneak my hand in to straighten out my ears after donning the helmet (my nickname as a kid was "Little Sails"). The N70 has larger air intakes on the crown and two extractors on the rear for ventilation coupled with a good-sized vent right in the bottom of the face shield. On my wife's kitchen scale the new Nolan in full dress (face shield and chin bar) weighed in at 3.7 lbs., which is where most Lexan

Polycarbonate shell helmets fall. With face shield, chin bar, and neck roll installed, I'd judge its quietness at speed to be about average when compared to full face helmets, but of course, it depends on which of the six helmet configurations you choose and what kind of windshield you have.

Apart from its versatility, I was also impressed with N70-2 GT's price. At about $360 for the Hi-Vis model ($10 more for graphics), to me this helmet merits a high "bang-for-buck" ranking. The N70-2 GT is available in two shell sizes, XS through XXXL and is comm system or emergency stop signal ready. For more information, visit https://www.nolan-usa.com/products/nolan-n70-2gt-touring-crossover-motorcycle-helmet-solid-color-dot.html.

Note: It only took two chocolate cookies to get my grandson, Keegan, to model the Nolan.

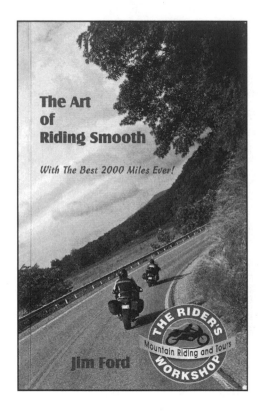

The Art
of
Riding Smooth

With The Best 2000 Miles Ever!

THE RIDER'S
Mountain Riding and Tours
WORKSHOP

Jim Ford

38

FOR THE FUN OF IT:
THE ART OF RIDING SMOOTH

There are lots of good books out there about riding motorcycles. In fact, author Jim Ford admits he had misgivings over what he could contribute to the body of knowledge already in print when friends urged him to write his own book. However, after reading his *The Art of Riding Smooth*, I think most riders would find this book an excellent step toward upgrading their skills and enhancing their experience on two wheels.

Ford certainly has all the credentials to qualify him as an authority on riding well. He has ridden nearly 600,000 miles (ninety-eight percent of those on the twisting "invisible roads" through the Appalachian Mountains) and has been conducting two-day tours and riding workshops on mountain roads that have garnered countless testimonials for more than ten years. In addition, Ford is an instrument-certified pilot with over twenty years of experience, which enhances his insight into the sport some call "the closest thing to flying."

Like most riding authorities, Ford puts great emphasis on safety in his book; however, one of his main premises is that riding safely is just one component of what he feels is the preeminent goal of riders: to have fun doing it! As a rider coach following his clients through serpentine side roads across the Appalachians, Ford has had a rich opportunity to diagnose the typical weaknesses riders may have that create dangerous scenarios. Not only has this given him compelling anecdotes to share with his readers, but it has also allowed him to create a collection of time-tested strategies to help riders stay out of trouble.

Although Ford's general riding philosophy (his license reads "ZEN") becomes clearer with each chapter of *The Art of Riding Smooth*, for me the real meat of the book was his breakdown and explanation of riding technique. As other readers have commented, Ford's discussions on factors like "vanishing points," acceleration, braking, up and downshifting, countersteering, and lean are clear and reinforced with captivating anecdotes. Although the book is easy reading, I found myself often pausing after a few pages to absorb a fresh take on technique, sometimes going back to reread sections in hopes of integrating a tip into my own riding. The only problem was I read it as the riding season here in Wisconsin was ending—I'm dying to try some of this stuff out!

A bonus feature of *The Art of Riding Smooth* is the final section called "The Magical Mountainous Tour." This sixty-page section is an invaluable guide to specific, little-trafficked routes through the Appalachians guaranteed to put Ford's techniques to the test and put wide grins on any rider's face. Ford also includes tips on points of interest to visit, historical background, and even directions to some of the best places to eat or stay.

Again, for Jim Ford, simply riding safely and incorporating good technique, though vitally important, are only pathways to the destination we all covet: enjoying the ride to the utmost. The love he conveys for confidently riding smoothly is infectious; reading his book will help any rider elevate both his or her skill and enjoyment.

The Art of Riding Smooth (190 pages, paperback) can be ordered through www.ridersworkshop.com and online booksellers.

39

EXPLORING THE
TWISTED ROAD

A few years ago, I attended a writing conference at a resort near Santa Fe, New Mexico. Except for a visit one night to the city's famed historic plaza, I didn't get time to see much of the area, but I was left thinking I'd like to return some day to learn more about Santa Fe's rich history and tour the mountains nearby. Reading all kinds of glowing accounts from riders in *BMW Owners News* about motorcycling in New Mexico whetted my desire for a return trip even more, so last April I took two weeks there. I would like to have taken a bike, but the thought of burning up tires crossing some of the mind numbing highways through Iowa, Missouri, Kansas, and Oklahoma had zero appeal. Then I came across Twisted Road.

Claiming to be "the fastest growing motorcycle sharing community on the planet," Twisted Road matches visitors to popular riding destinations with cycle owners interested in renting their bikes. The online rental service is the brainchild of Austin Rothbard, who, after twenty years in the corporate world, founded Twisted Road in 2017, working out of his kids' playroom. Since then, the web-based outfit's staff has grown to five work-from-home employees who provide customer service to over 100,000 subscribers, both renters and bike owners.

Rothbard said building the company's online presence was "like nurturing a baby." Twisted Road's product is the service the website provides, so careful attention had to be given to ease of use, communication and accountability. I found the process of finding and setting up a rental was very user-friendly and seamless. Santa Fe is a 400-year-old city, and once I arrived at my casita in the heart of it, I was concerned about navigating the winding narrow streets while slaloming around the hundreds of tourists glued to their cell phones (sidewalks vary from a foot wide to non-existent). I needn't have worried, though, since the owner of the bike I chose graciously dropped off and picked up his F 650 GS and gave me all kinds of pointers on how to clear the city to get to the best ride routes, one of which was the area's legendary "High Road to Taos."

Austin Rothbard said one of the biggest keys to Twisted Road's success is the motorcyclist community itself. "This community is really, really cool!" said Rothbard. "The bike owners want to see you have fun with their favorite toy. Nine out of ten times owners will hop into their cars and resolve any issues during a rental." Of the thousands of customer reviews on the Twisted Road site, Rothbard claims ninety-eight percent of them carry five-star ratings.

On one of the days I was to use the GS, wind gusts of up to sixty-five miles per hour were predicted, but by contacting Twisted Road, the owner and I were able to modify the rental agreement with the 24-7 on-call help from Clare, one of their customer service agents—this on a Sunday night at 8PM! I had no other issues during my rental experience except for catching something in my eye on a mountain route that cut short one jaunt. Twisted Road vets both owners and renters and hasn't yet had a problem they haven't been able to resolve. Rothbard told me about one rider from Iceland who was on a quest to circle the world and who wanted to rent a 1200 GS Adventure in Washington DC and ride to San Francisco. The rider said he would cover the cost of shipping the bike back to DC, but (no surprise to MOA-ers) the owner wanted to fly out and ride it home. "This community never ceases to amaze me!" said Rothbard.

In addition to the rental service, Twisted Road recently added an "Events" tab on their site where riders can get a free listing of most rallies and moto-gatherings in whatever area they're visiting. In their "One, Two, Free" promotion, riders can get a free, one-day rental after their second rental. Rates for renting their bikes through Twisted Road are set by owners, and the more bikes available in a specific city, the lower the rates. The GS I rented costed $123 a day plus insurance (which Twisted Road offers) and a community fee; however, I noticed in a city like Los Angeles, bikes could be rented for as little as sixty-five dollars a day, many BMWs and some Zero electrics.

A rental service like Twisted Road provides not only a way to get some saddle time while traveling but also an opportunity to try a bike you may be looking at buying. For owners, it's a chance to earn some money when their bikes are sitting idle. Whichever position you're in, I recommend giving renting a try.

For more information, visit TwistedRoad.com.

OFF THE ROAD

Though the next four stories only deal tangentially with motorcycling, they've received favorable comments from both riders and non-riders. "Get A Job" and "Two Days on the Eau Claire" were featured on Wisconsin Public Radio's "Wisconsin Life;" the other two have never been published before.

40

GET A JOB
THE REAL WORLD OF WORK
RAISES ITS UGLY HEAD . . .

All through high school I played drums in a band that by my junior year was doing one or two gigs across the state every weekend. We were definitely making money (despite the sixteen percent that went to an agent), but playing out was less a job and more a lark most of the time, although it did give us non-athletes some high school status we never could have earned normally. We sank practically everything we made into more and more expensive equipment and other stuff that now could be considered pretty frivolous: leather-fringed vests, towering piles of $33^{1/3}$ albums, and completely impractical vehicles like broken-down Honda motorcycles.

However, by the tail end of my senior year, the band had, well, disbanded, and after watching me sleep late, loll in front of the TV watching cartoons and eating potato chips, my dad said, "Enough! Why don't you have a job?" He pointed to a Help Wanted classified for a delivery person at Pizza Villa.

I must admit that at the ripe old age of seventeen I was pretty naïve about the working world. As I was offered the job, it was somehow of little concern to me that the conditions for working at Pizza Villa meant that (A) I was required to use my own car, (B) I had to pay for my own gas, and (C) I would be "off the clock" when making deliveries (although I would be paid a whopping fifty cents for every stop).

The car requirement didn't bother me, since I knew my dad was so anxious to see me learn the real meaning of work, he would let me use his. But more importantly, somehow I had created this ridiculous fantasy of what a cool job delivering pizzas would be. I imagined myself tearing around the city like Steve McQueen in *Bullitt*, negligee-clad divorcees greeting me at every door. I could see my pockets stuffed with wads of tip cash from the town's country club royalty, who I assumed breathlessly longed to have greasy pizzas brought to them by willing serfs like me. I saw myself as the hit of cheerleader slumber parties—could I come in and stay a while?

Okay, I was wrong.

The first night I was to be "trained" by Don (also known as "Smoke") who was working his last night. After loading up pizzas into the slots of the portable oven (more about this later) we cruised through town in his rust-pocked Ford Fairlane, windows open and the sparks from his perpetual Camels shooting straight into the back seat. He explained how he was accepting an understanding judge's generous offer to allow his enlistment in the army as a suitable alternative to serving sixty days in jail for a little matter involving a substantial number of missing cases of beer and vodka from his previous job. Yes, things like that happened in the '60s. Through squinted eyes as he lit another Camel with the dash lighter, Smoke gave forth a lengthy critique on the physical merits of the two high school girls who worked in the Villa's kitchen and why, for some reason, they had "their noses up their butts" when it came to him, despite his constant leering.

On the first delivery, Don had me accompany him to the door of one side of a sad-looking duplex. I carried the pizza box to a young woman in sweat pants who struggled to keep three or four urchins from spilling out the door. Don collected the money—"No tip," he said. Back at the Villa, I estimated this single delivery had consumed ten miles and almost a half hour of Don's ancient Fairlane's remaining life, making me wonder, even with my primitive understanding of economics, if fifty cents represented any amount of profit. But I soldiered on and returned the next night for my first solo runs.

As I said, a big part of my initial attraction to the job was the unrestricted use of my dad's car. He had a powder blue Volkswagen Karmann Ghia, which wasn't a muscle car like the GTOs, Road Runners, and Super Bees that were popular then, but came close to passing as a real sports car—small, sleek, bucket seats, low to the ground, with rack and pinion steering and four on the floor. When dared, under the right conditions and some deft clutch and gas work, I could even get it to chirp going into second gear. The main pastime in my hometown then was "making laps," driving up and down Main Street in the evening, so scratching away from traffic lights and around corners in the Karmann Ghia had its social appeal. And I had come to the realization that the only way I could make my fifty-cent commissions profitable was to drive as fast as possible.

Unfortunately, "spirited driving" did not work well with Pizza Villa's solution for keeping its pizzas warm. I was given a stainless-steel cube about three-by-three feet with a door on one side and a compartment for a heating source on the other. The heater was a can of Sterno, which I'm not sure is available anymore. Sterno fuel was a kind of jellied alcohol that, once lit, turned to liquid. I wedged the pizza box monstrosity onto the passenger seat of the Volkswagen with the door facing out, so I could load and remove the pizza boxes. But as I revved the rear mounted engine and drifted around the first right hand turn, I realized this caused the burning Sterno fuel to slosh out of the oven and onto the emergency brake lever, the shifter, and my lap. Imagine careening down a city street while simultaneously trying to tamp out undulating blue flames. Of course, I could have stopped, but that would endanger my crude estimation of profit-loss. Luckily, there was no obvious damage to the car or my bathing suit parts, although people frequently sniffed in my presence, probably wondering exactly what kind of petroleum product I was using for after shave. After that first night, I took care to cut the cake of Sterno fuel in half to at least reduce the chance of spills.

As the reader can guess, my fantasies about being a delivery guy never came close to materializing. Tips were few and far between, and most often, no customers ever tried to seduce me—instead I was usually greeted by bedraggled baby sitters, groups of half-drunk college age guys, and/or kids thrusting some change and few bucks at me (exact amount) and grabbing the greasy pizza carton. Then, of course, there were the dark, rainy nights when I forlornly searched for often missing house numbers, the prank calls where I made nothing, and the messed up orders—"We said NO pepperoni!" Some nights were interminably slow, with nothing better to do than chat up the two high school girls behind the counter, who showed no more interest in me than they had Don.

After two weeks of misery, I would roll home after midnight, only to have nightmares about phantom addresses, screaming customers, and dark streets leading nowhere. It was about then that Mike, one of my band mates, called to invite me on a road trip to Alabama to see his grandparents, with a possible side trip to Panama City to swim in the Gulf. I gave Pizza Villa my notice, and not surprisingly, when we got back, I heard they had closed, and my dad again started scanning the want ads.

41

PHYSICAL EDUCATION

WHAT BETTER PREPARATION FOR LIFE IN 1969 THAN HIGH SCHOOL GYM CLASS?

I remember it was kind of chilly that morning. I guess the heat hadn't been on that long, and of course, we were all standing around in our regulation blue gym shorts and grimy T-shirts. Since it was 1969, girls had their own, separate class. Despite our leering and clever taunts, they trotted by in their little one-piece outfits, conspicuously ignoring us, and took up station about a mile away at the other end of the fieldhouse. Anyway, chilly. But sunny, too. My high school's fieldhouse, where we had gym, was enormous, probably one of the biggest in the state, and had these tall windows high up above the balconies that gave the place an expansive, cathedral-like feeling. It made you feel small, but with the early morning sun streaming in, it was actually kind of nice to be running around in shorts, when a half hour ago you might have been been trudging to school through January's snow and slush.

The first thing we had to do was line up on our numbers. Apparently, there were simply too many of us for somebody with what we felt was Coach Gronsky's limited mental capacity to recognize by face, so we all stood on our special number painted in white on the floor, and he came around with his red book to mark down the vacant numbers. We'd often trade around and even openly moved sometimes to cover the number of a guy who was skipping, but it didn't seem to make much difference. Phys Ed was a big joke to most of us; we were all seniors and had grown pretty contemptuous of the whole high school routine, although we were clueless on what might be coming next.

Unless they had been caught drinking, all the decent athletes were out for a sport, so of course, they didn't have to take gym. They'd hang out in the coach's office or down, under the stage in the equipment room acting tough and generally sneering at our class, which was mostly made up of long-haired goof-offs, nerds, hoods, and guys so far down the social ladder there wasn't even a term for them.

Anyway, while Gronsky was taking roll we'd seize the opportunity to fool around, you know, pulling a guy's shorts down from behind (you might want to wait until the girls' class was trotting by, of course), fart noises, burping, the usual kind of high class entertainment we were generally known for. Once roll was taken, Gronsky was already a little peeved, so he started barking at us to get down to the day's work. At that point we were in the annual gymnastics unit, and Gronsky grunted out some unintelligible stuff about "vaulting the pommel horse." Now understand, we didn't get to use the real pommel horse; that was reserved for the real athletes on the gymnastics team. We got this facsimile of a pommel horse, or maybe, judging from the way it looked, it was the original pommel horse. It was only a foot or two long, a foot thick, and supported about five feet off the floor by two black, iron legs attached to a spreading base. It was leather, only the stiching had come undone in places, and whatever was left of the horse hair stuffing was hanging out at the seams. The horse looked like a section of a big, beat up tootsie roll.

Though "pommel horse" and even "vaulting" were new additions to my vocabulary, I gathered the idea was we were supposed to run at the horse full tilt for about ten yards, bounce on this wooden trampoline thing, and sort of leap frog over the horse lengthwise. Gronsky explained it in about three words then had us line up to go one at a time. Well, as you might imagine, no one was taking it too seriously, but we played along, since it was better than climbing the ropes, the activity where Ted Ambrose had almost gotten killed a couple days earlier; but that's another story. After you did it, which, it turned out, wasn't too hard, you were supposed to go to the back of the line and wait for your next turn. But after I took my first turn I noticed something: Frank Blouderman had been in back of me before, and now he was in front of me, only I had never seen him vault.

I had been mildly curious about watching Frank try it, because Frank probably went 250 plus pounds, with maybe one or two pounds of that being muscle. Along with probably every other kid in class, I couldn't help wondering how he was going to get over that horse. As the line moved around for my next turn, I watched Frank. When he got close to the front, he shuffled around, eased out of line, and went to the back, on the other side from Gronsky, obviously hoping his 300 pounds of Hostess Twinkie would blend in with the rest of us knobby-kneed weaklings. I think pretty soon everybody was aware of what Frank was doing, but nobody said anything, which was unusual, because most of time the guys in my gym class would have stood in line to prey on somebody that might be showing some kind of weakness. But maybe it was because it was so elementary, I mean, it was physics: no way was Frank ever going over that horse. Possibly this was what Physical Education was all about.

But Gronsky caught on. "BLOUDERMAN! FRONT OF THE LINE!" Frank looked down like maybe if he didn't acknowledge Gronsky, he'd go away. "BLOUDERMAN! GET YOUR BIG BUTT DOWN HERE AND GET OVER THAT HORSE!" Granted, Gronsky wasn't exactly known for his sensitivity, but what did he think? No way was Frank going over that horse, unless Gronsky planned on giving him wings or rockets or something. But Frank sheepishly gave in and came up to the front of the line. My class had been slow to warm up to this opportunity to victimize somebody, but they quickly picked up the spirit from Gronsky and started saying sarcastic stuff like, "Come on, Frank, go get 'em!" and "Yeah, Frank, get your big butt over that horse!" This was greeted by big laughs, of course. Frank, by now, looked pretty close to tears. He was about on the bottom of the totem pole, anyway, in gym and had already taken a lot of serious teasing for having to be forced to take a shower with us. (Apparently he had some kind of operation scar he wasn't too keen on showing us.) This had the potential for blowing away any shred of self-respect he might have left.

But then, he seemed to undergo a transformation. Gronsky was barking things like, "COME ON FRANK, WE'RE WAAAAAITING!" and Frank wasn't listening to Gronsky or the rest of us, just sort of staring down the runway at the stupid horse, like it was his destiny or something. He looked like he might have been telling himself, "Hey, maybe I can do this. After all, Gronsky is the teacher; he wouldn't make me do this if he didn't think I could, would he?" Or possibly Frank was thinking this was a convenient way of killing himself. Anyway, he seemed to bunch himself up, and then he started off.

Frank was not what you'd call a quick person. But he did start to pick up a little speed as he rolled on down toward that horse. You couldn't deny he sure looked like he had a lot of momentum. Everybody was quiet now, it was like watching somebody on the trapeze or that moment when I had watched Evel Knieval revving his Triumph T100 before he attempted to jump a fountain at Caesar's Palace. When Frank hit that little springboard full bore, it slapped to the floor and never came up. Frank didn't even seem to try to jump but just kept sailing at the same height right into the blunt end of the horse. There was kind of a dull, smacking noise as Frank and the horse met. The horse didn't budge, of course, it being all cast iron and probably bolted to the floor, for all I know. Frank tipped over sideways and slowly began curling himself around this basketball-sized welt growing on his belly. The fieldhouse was silent for a moment, then somebody quietly said, "Way to go, Frank." As you'd probably guess, everybody exploded into hysterics, being our usual compassionate selves, although a couple guys did edge over to make sure Frank was still alive. Gronsky was trying to suppress a grin—you could tell he was trying to hold back. He rolled his eyes and mumbled, "All right, Blouderman, get out of the way, go sit on the bleachers." (Sitting on the bleachers was Gronsky's cure-all for any injury in gym, as I would personally find out later in the wrestling unit.)

A little later, when Gronsky started bellowing something about laps and showers, my friend, Steve, and I went over to see how Frank was doing. We asked the standard, "Are you okay?" He was bent over, with his face in his hands, and nodded that he was, but you could tell he didn't want anybody to help him or even look at him, since it was plain he had been crying, probably the worst thing a guy could do in gym. I felt sorry for him. I really did. But it didn't stop me from joking around in the locker room with the rest of the guys later as we hid yet one more poor soul's underwear while he was in the shower.

About forty years later, I now suspect that those laughs came less from cruelty and more from a mixture of nervous relief and apprehension. In those days, we carefully avoided talking about the prospects that were haunting our near futures: Join our dads at the paper mill? Move away from home? The draft? Vietnam? Whether we recognized it then or not, that gym class had actually been an education. We hadn't been Frank Blouderman this time, but we suspected our futures would probably hold a day when we could be.

42

A Favorite Tree

Giving Voices to Our Silent Friends

A few weeks ago a friend posted a photo online of his "favorite tree," a magnificent sugar maple in his front yard, probably five feet around. In response, I posted one of my own favorites, and soon friends and family were doing likewise. It got me to thinking: does everybody have a favorite tree? I really hope so.

On our little chunk of property in the township of Scandinavia, we have thousands of trees. When we first moved here it was almost solid with thirty- or forty-year-old aspen. Most were about five or six stories tall, only leafing out at the top, since we live on the north side of a ridge. Our gloomy woods had little to no understory and scarce wildlife, other than an occasional family of whitetails wandering through or a bunch of flying squirrels who liked the holes chipped out by

Pileated Woodpeckers. When a ferocious straight line wind uprooted and sheared some of them off twenty years ago, we had the land logged.

What sprang up next was a cornucopia of species: ash, red and white oak, birch, basswood, silver maple, a few cherry, and of course, more aspen. An army of wildlife also moved in to feast on seedlings, buds, raspberries, and hazelnuts. Now our little plot is once again solid with trees, making it hard to pick a favorite. It might just be the lonely, towering white pine that stands directly in front of our house. It's got to be almost a hundred years old and is one of only a few ancients on the ridge that were left, either for seed or because they weren't prime stock (ours has a double trunk). The broad bottom branches of our pine used to fan out to the ground, making a cool, damp tent. My neighbor, Roy, told me when he was a boy, he'd frequently be sent to fetch their blind cow from beneath its branches, the poor animal lurching around in endless circles.

But my favorite could also be the scraggly paper birch in the fencerow across the road. Over the years we've lived here it has resolutely endured blizzards, ice storms, sieges of wild grape and leaf curl, the continual encroachment of the farmer's reach, and the yearly assaults from bucks sharpening up their antlers. We occasionally have a few grouse around, which you can sometimes see silhouetted in the birch's branches, probably hunting for its buds or maybe, as the old timers in the neighborhood contend, sitting out their hangovers from eating grapes fermented on the vine. I can't help but admire that little tree's pluck.

On the other hand, maybe it's the white oak I sit in every gun deer season. It pokes up like a ship's mainmast near the top of the ridge, a self-righteous, indignant taunt to lightening. Sitting up there in November, I can scan five miles of snowy countryside, a patchwork quilt of harvested corn fields, woodlots, and swamp. Squirrels like that tree, anyway, and will scurry up and down, keeping the trunk between us, sometimes peeking around to wonder at the curious creature shivering away, cloaked in blaze orange.

We're tree-rich in Wisconsin. Millions upon billions of trees, each one a brave, but silent testament to tenaciousness. Maybe by choosing favorites, our lives, as Shakespeare wrote, give them tongues. Tongues to tell their stories, as well as our own.

43
TWO DAYS ON THE EAU CLAIRE

"No man ever steps in the same river twice, for it's not the same river and he's not the same man."—Heraclitus

Back in 1972 I was a sophomore at the University of Wisconsin—Eau Claire. Like many at that time, I was pretty clueless about what direction my life would take, just happy enough to be in college and not Vietnam or working a grueling paper mill job, like many of my buddies. A high lottery number (344) had saved me from the draft, and a small inheritance from my grandmother had paid some of my tuition. One thing I did know, though, was that I ached to fish, desperate to find a place where a poor, boat-less college kid could escape stuffy classrooms and a house full of obnoxious roommates, maybe to catch a smallmouth bass.

On the off chance I'd meet some winsome English majors, I had joined the staff of the campus literary magazine. It was a position breathtaking in its insignificance, and I found the staff to be all male and all as questionably-intentioned as myself, but our office was shared with the magazine's advisor, a promising young professor named Bruce Taylor. Taylor, an angler like myself, drew me a map of a "secret" stretch of the Eau Claire River I could access with my old Honda CB350. So, on a crisp, early fall day, armed with a cheap spinning rod bungeed to my sissy bar and a dinky tackle box strapped across my saddle, I followed a labyrinth of county and township roads to a dirt path leading down to a secluded section of the river.

The Eau Claire River (one of two in Wisconsin) flows southwest from northern Wisconsin down to a confluence with the Chippewa, which then joins the Mississippi. In the last half of the nineteenth century, both the Chippewa and the Eau Claire were major means of transporting logs from the great Wisconsin Pinery down to Eau Claire, the city, which was nicknamed "Sawdust City." Although "Eau Claire" means "clear water" in French, and a glass of it will appear pure, the river is actually stained brown with the tannic acid it picks up flowing through tamarack swamps to the north.

This section of the Eau Claire didn't look too promising, just a slow rolling, open pool about thirty yards wide with none of the usual spillways, rock banks, and roiling currents you'd commonly associate with smallies. A canopy of overhanging oaks and ashes kept the pool blanketed in shadow. I waded in, confident my tennies and jeans would dry on the ride home, and the chilled water coursed around my legs, as Jim Harrison once wrote, "at the exact but varying speed of life."

I made a few fruitless casts with a silver spoon, letting it tumble to a few feet off the bottom and then jigging it in, but soon I ran into trouble with a line snarl. My lure sank to the bottom of the river, probably I figured, to be lost on a rock or submerged log. Once I got the line untangled, I started to reel in and, as expected, felt stiff resistance. But then the line moved—a fish! It was a classic battle, the smallmouth turning the tranquil pool into a circus of sprints and breeching belly-flops. The big-shouldered fish eventually tired, and I lipped him, removed the hook and gently lowered him into the root beer-colored water. Thank you, Dr. Taylor!

Almost fifty years later, after a long career spent away from Eau Claire teaching and writing for motorcycle magazines, I had retired and moved back. Once again, I found myself jones-ing for some piscatorial action. Larry Stordahl, an old friend and self-appointed tour guide to the Chippewa Valley, had taken me around to a few places on the Eau Claire he thought I could wade and possibly have some luck, one just down the bank from an old Uniroyal tire factory in the middle of the city, now being gentrified into condos, tech startups, and artist studios. On a sticky July morning, a week later, I decided to give it a try.

Decked out in my fancy chest waders, carbide-studded boots, fly fishing vest, and a preposterous, caped hat, I felt a little self-conscious as I left my car, waited for traffic to clear, and crossed a city street. A deer fly patch stuck to the cap with a few carcasses from the past seasons made the image even more glamorous. I tried to edge my way down the steep, rocky bank sideways but wound up hobbling, stumbling, and finally gracelessly skidding on my butt down to the shoreline. As I waded in I was given even more evidence that I wasn't the agile twenty-one-year-old anymore, teetering my way through a treacherous jumble of sharp, slippery rocks and chunks of concrete hiding in the dark water. My wading staff left back home, I retreated to search for a branch or piece of driftwood I could substitute, and once equipped and feeling a little safer, I cautiously worked the river a little with a floating Rapala.

Even though I was just a few hundred yards up from the Dewey Street Bridge, the steep slopes, covered with lush greenery and flood-worn rock outcroppings, made for a fairly unspoiled pastoral scene and cut me off from city life, other than the occasional honks and Harley revs that percolated through to break the spell. Of course, the banks weren't exactly pristine, strewn with a few water bottles, some poor soul's underwear, and the ubiquitous white plastic bags, but I was there for fishing, not a nature walk.

After a few hours of fighting the prospect of tripping and winding up struggling to free myself from water-filled waders as I floated through the center of the city, I found a spit of sand that reached a ways out, where I could cast into a seam in the current. A medium-sized smallmouth soon hit and gave me a nice fight as I played it up to the shore, a lovely, bronze-backed fish, which angrily darted back into the depths after being released.

The sun had cleared the treetops by then, and swaddled in my gear, the heat had me breathing hard and swimming in sweat. Although I usually scoff at the way everyone seems to carry water bottles now, I cursed myself for not bringing one. I thought about things like heat stroke, wrenched knees, back spasms, my cell phone left in the car—old man worries that made me surrender and set to clawing my way on all fours back up to civilization.

In the car with the air conditioning on full blast, I reflected that, as far as fishing goes, the morning's outing could be called a success, and I was glad I did it, although my doddering struggles had been fairly sobering. More and more often, I find I have to reconcile with myself that I just can't do things like this little fishing expedition like I used to, at least not as well, but I guess I should count myself lucky to do them at all. I suppose you could say the Eau Claire was the same river I had found in my college days, at least in name, but I definitely wasn't the same man. Nonetheless, though, as Harrison also wrote, the advancing years can kick you brutally hard, fishing a river, "you forget the kick."

AND ONE MORE . . .

44

A Rider Writes: Dilemma

It seems like whenever I meet someone new these days, I invariably get the question, "Are you retired?" I guess I look like I should be. But even though it's been a few years since I worked full time as a teacher, I respond, "Semi-retired." This of course, leads to the question, "Oh, what do you do now?" After more than twenty years of publishing stories, features, profiles, news stories, and now two books, I've decided I'm entitled to saying, "I'm a writer." And therein lies the rub.

When dental hygienists, new neighbors, coffee shop friends learn I'm a writer, my questioners' interest peaks; maybe they're imagining they've finally met a successful novelist, screenwriter, or at least, a poet. So they ask, "What do you write?" When I reply I write about motorcycling, the peaks become valleys. What so often follows is a story about their brother, aunt, uncle, or friend who was hurt in a cycle accident. Their solemn expression and a slight narrowing of the eyes gives me the feeling they've somehow lumped me into the list of people who are to blame.

For instance, a few weeks ago my wife and I attended a homecoming game at our alma mater. Surprised by the packed stadium, we were lucky to be graciously invited to sit in the Hall of Fame section (again, probably because I look old). Rest assured, there was nothing I accomplished during my college career that would qualify me for that honor, other than doing my part to keep the Walters Beer company in business.

Anyway, as we watched the mighty Eau Claire Blugolds get creamed by an enormous crew from UW-River Falls, who obviously spent their spare time throwing tractors back and forth, I struck up a conversation with a man next to me (a genuine Hall of Famer in football, class of '71). It was one of those glorious, blue bird sky afternoons in Wisconsin— everyone pink-cheeked and sweatered, marching band, cheerleaders wearing mittens and stocking caps, brats grilling on tailgates—but then the conversation took a cloudy, unfortunate script. Once he described how his son's Harley had gotten compressed to half its length in a rear-ender, the poor kid enduring seven surgeries, the conversation slowly drowned into a pool of niceties.

I get it. There is no denying bikes are dangerous. No amount of mitigations like training, safety gear, or vigilance will ever totally erase that fact. Although I have gone down a few times, I've never been in what I'd call an accident, but there was one incident where I was close to those who had. I suppose it's revealing that I've never written about it before . . .

Back when I was still in college, two of my cycling buddies and I headed down to Madison one weekend in early spring to visit friends. "B.A." was on a CB450 and had recently returned from a long tour out west. Out of college and a few years older, B.A. loomed large to me and my roommates. He would drop in now and then to crash on our couch or share his latest exploits. His goal was to make enough money harvesting carp on Lake Pepin from his sailboat to eventually get a big enough boat to sail the Caribbean. If it was raining, he was the kind of guy who preferred stepping outside in his boxers to wash up instead of using our shower.

On the other bike, another 450, was Ralph, one of my roommates. He was a guy Kerouac would describe as a "holy goof." Six foot three, incapable of doing anything quietly, a bushel of curly red hair, aviator glasses, perpetual broad smile, and always up for anything at any time of day, he dearly loved motorcycles, even after breaking his collar bone when he hit a culvert on his Suzuki dirt bike.

Both B.A. and Ralph had their girlfriends with them, while I was riding solo. We split up in Madison but were to meet up on a Saturday afternoon at a pal's apartment for a party. Soon after the party started, our host said there was a call for me. It was Ralph, and his usually booming voice sounded shaky. His call was sketchy on details, for Ralph was already on some pain killers, but he explained that on the way over, an elderly woman had run a stop sign and hit all four of them. He knew his leg was broken (two compound fractures, I found out later), and his pillion had hip and leg fractures. The other couple (they had been riding two abreast) took less of an impact, but also had leg injuries and various bumps, scrapes, and bruises. Both bikes were totaled.

I remember feeling faint and having to slide down the wall and sit on the floor, carefree weekend romp suddenly turning to tragedy in seconds. As I left my friends at the university hospital and returned home alone the next day, the weather had turned bitterly cold and windy, seemingly a reflection of my dour spirits. That summer, Ralph stayed at school for summer classes, and I decided to stay with him, doing the best I could to be his step-and-fetch-it, as he crutched around in a full leg cast.

I was still riding my hot-rodded Honda 350, but its presence in our driveway didn't hold the allure it once did for either of us. One night in July, it was stolen. The thieves had tried to hot wire it to no avail and then stripped it and pushed it down a railroad embankment. Insurance helped somewhat to put it back together, but I sold it soon after, and probably to pre-empt my getting another bike, my dad gave me his used AMC Gremlin. Ralph and I ran the tires off it in August on a frantic trip to California, which included a night sleeping in Big Sur and an ill-advised climb down to the beach, where Ralph destroyed his second walking cast.

I was off bikes for a few years until I ran across a Honda dealer going out of business and practically giving away bikes. I couldn't resist a shiny red XL175 at cost (I told my wife it was strictly for commuting, a hedge against 1979's gas crisis), and so started the revolving door of bike purchases and road adventures leading up to the present.

I guess, as a moto-writer, I'm a little ambivalent, in no small part due to the unfortunate stories I've heard and my own experience with accidents. I share a passion for motorcycling of just about any kind, and to this day, a bike going by will always command my attention, but I don't purposefully try to talk anyone into buying a motorcycle. I'm reluctant to invite anyone to take a ride on the back. I did once give one of my grandsons a set of ten toy cycles, only to notice they had disappeared the next time I saw him, and since my daughter-in-law is an ER nurse anesthetist, I can guess why. And when someone has that gleam in their eyes and mentions they're thinking of taking up riding, I try to remain stoically indifferent.

I will say this: being a motorcyclist has opened a world I otherwise never would have known. It is a good one. And I have to mention here that not everyone I meet has gloomy stories of accidents when it comes to motorcycles. I've talked to vets who have said riding a cycle has been their favorite therapy. I've talked to couples who get a faraway look in their eyes as they recount a cross-country trip they took on a Gold Wing. I've met lots of men and women my age who fondly look back to their days on Triumphs, Nortons, Harleys, Yamahas, or even little Rupp mini-bikes. And I've heard plenty of former riders damn the day they had to hang up their helmets for good. When I'm filling up my gas tank and spot someone walking over, I look forward to the "cycle talk" I know is about to begin.

Should I unapologetically tell stories about the visceral joy of cleanly slicing through a sweeper or tilting through a twistie? Should I dare to try to describe to others how I love the gentle, deep-throated thrum of an oil-headed GS or the snarl of a rat bike? Will I continue to write about the closest I'll ever come to flying?

In a word . . . yup.

Acknowledgements

I especially want to thank my publisher, Mike Fitterling of Road Dog Publications, for his patience, expertise and advice that made this project a painless affair. Special thanks to my wife, Deb, who, upon entering my office when I was working, graciously ignored (usually) my best impression of a grumpy old man, and to my kids, Kellen and Sarah. Also, thanks to Bill Wiegand, Maureen McCollum, Darrell Broten, Mark Barnes, Erika Janik, Peter Egan, Al Ross, Roger Holman, Ralph Barsema, Jack Riepe, Dave Johnson, and Andy Goldfine for their advice and support. Lastly, thanks to Keegan Davis for his modeling talent and to Ross Olson for reviving a painful memory by finding me a photo of the back seat from a 1964 Ford Mustang.

-Ron Davis 12/23/21

Other Books from Road Dog Publications

Those Two Idiots![1 2] by A. P. Atkinson
Mayhem, mirth, and adventure follow two riders across two continents. Setting off for Thailand thinking they were prepared, this story if full of mishaps and triumphs. An honest journey with all the highs and lows, wins and losses, wonderful people and low-lifes, and charms and pitfalls of the countries traveled through.

Motorcycles, Life, and . . . [1 2] by Brent Allen
Sit down at a table and talk motorcycles, life and . . . (fill in the blank) with award winning riding instructor and creator of the popular "Howzit Done?" video series, Brent "Capt. Crash" Allen. Here are his thoughts about riding and life and how they combine told in a lighthearted tone.

The Elemental Motorcyclist[1 2] by Brent Allen
Brent's second book offers more insights into life and riding and how they go together. This volume, while still told in the author's typical easy-going tone, gets down to more specifics about being a better rider.

A Short Ride in the Jungle[1 2] by Antonia Bolingbroke-Kent
A young woman tackles the famed Ho Chi Minh Trail alone on a diminutive pink Honda Cub armed only with her love of Southeast Asia, its people, and her wits.

Mini Escapades around the British Isles[1 2] by Zoë Cano
As a wonderful compilation of original short stories closer to home, Zoë Cano captures the very essence of Britain's natural beauty with eclectic travels she's taken over the years exploring England, Ireland, Scotland, and Wales.

Bonneville Go or Bust[1 2] by Zoë Cano
A true story with a difference. Zoë had no experience for such a mammoth adventure of a lifetime but goes all out to make her dream come true to travel solo across the lesser known roads of the American continent on a classic motorcycle.

I loved reading this book. She has a way of putting you right into the scene. It was like riding on the back seat and experiencing this adventure along with Zoë. —★★★★ Amazon Review

Southern Escapades[1][2] by Zoë Cano

As an encore to her cross country trip, Zoë rides along the tropical Gulf of México and Atlantic Coast in Florida, through the forgotten backroads of Alabama and Georgia. This adventure uncovers the many hidden gems of lesser known places in these beautiful Southern states.

. . . Zoë has once again interested and entertained me with her American adventures. Her insightful prose is a delight to read and makes me want to visit the same places.—★★★★★ Amazon Review

Chilli, Skulls & Tequila[1][2] by Zoë Cano

Zoe captures the spirit of beautiful Baja California, México, with a solo 3 000 mile adventure encountering a myriad of surprises along the way and unique, out-of-the-way places tucked into Baja's forgotten corners.

Zoe adds hot chilli and spices to her stories, creating a truly mouth-watering reader's feast!—★★★★ Amazon Review

Hellbent for Paradise[1][2] by Zoë Cano

The inspiring—and often nail-biting—tale of Zoë's exploits roaming the jaw-dropping natural wonders of New Zealand on a mission to find her own paradise.

Mini Escapades around the British Isles[1][2] by Zoë Cano

As a wonderful compilation of original short stories closer to home, Zoë Cano captures the very essence of Britain's natural beauty with eclectic travels she's taken over the years exploring England, Ireland, Scotland, and Wales.

Shiny Side Up[1][2] by Ron Davis

A delightful collection of essays and articles from Ron Davis, Associate Editor and columnist for *BMW Owners News*. This book is filled with tales of the road and recounts the joys and foibles of motorcycle ownership and maintenance. Read it and find out why Ron is a favorite of readers of the *Owners News*!

Beads in the Headlight [1] by Isabel Dyson

A British couple tackle riding from Alaska to Tierra del Fuego two-up on a 31 year-old BMW "airhead." Join them on this epic journey across two continents.

A great blend of travel, motorcycling, determination, and humor. —★★★★★ Amazon Review

Chasing America [1] [2] by Tracy Farr

Tracy Farr sets off on multiple legs of a motorcycle ride to the four corners of America in search of the essence of the land and its people.

In Search of Greener Grass [1] by Graham Field

With game show winnings and his KLR 650, Graham sets out solo for Mongolia & beyond. Foreword by Ted Simon

Eureka [1] by Graham Field

Graham sets out on a journey to Kazahkstan only to realize his contrived goal is not making him happy. He has a "Eureka!" moment, turns around, and begins to enjoy the ride as the ride itself becomes the destination.

Different Natures [1] by Graham Field

The story of two early journeys Graham made while living in the US, one north to Alaska and the other south through México. Follow along as Graham tells the stories in his own unique way.

Thoughts on the Road [1] [2] by Michael Fitterling

The Editor of *Vintage Japanese Motorcycle Magazine* ponders his experiences with motorcycles and riding and how they've intersected and influenced his life.

Northeast by Northwest [1] [2] by Michael Fitterling

The author finds two motorcycle journeys of immense help staving off depression and the other effects of stress. Along the way, he discovers the beauty of North America and the kindness of its people.

. . . one of t.he most captivating stories I have read in a long time. Truly a MUST read!!—★★★★★ Amazon Review

Hit the Road, Jac! [1][2] *by Jacqui Furneaux*
At 50, Jacqui leaves her home and family, buys a motorcycle in India, and begins a seven-year world-wide journey with no particular plan. Along the way she comes to terms with herself and her family.

Asphalt & Dirt [1][2] *by Aaron Heinrich*
A compilation of profiles of both famous figures in the motorcycle industry and relatively unknown people who ride, dispelling the myth of the stereotypical "biker" image.

The Dog, The Hog, & the Iron Horse [1][2] *by Alex Kendall*
An Englishman seeks out the "real" America and Americans on three trips across the US; one by bus, east to west; another by train west to east; and finally on an iconic Harley-Davidson motorcycle from north to south. Inspired by "beat" writers, join Alex on his exploration of this land of Kerouac and Thompson.

Chasing Northern Lights [1][2] *by Miguel Oldenburg*
An immigrant from Venezuela and new citizen of the Untied States sets off for Alaska to get to know more about his adopted home and fellow Americans.

The Tom Report [1][2] *by Tom Reuter*
Two young men set out from Washinton state on Suzuki DR650 dual sport motorcycles. Join them and a colorful cast of fellow travelers as they wind their way south to the end of the world. Their journey is filled with fun, danger, and even enlightenment.

A Tale of Two Dusters & Other Stories [1][2] *by Kirk Swanick*
In this collection of tales, Kirk Swanick tells of growing up a gearhead behind both the wheels of muscle cars and the handlebars of motorcycles and describes the joys and trials of riding

Man in the Saddle [1][2] *by Paul van Hoof*
Aboard a 1975 Moto Guzzi V7, Paul starts out from Alaska for Ushuaia. Along the way there are many twists and turns, some which change his life forever. English translation from the original Dutch.